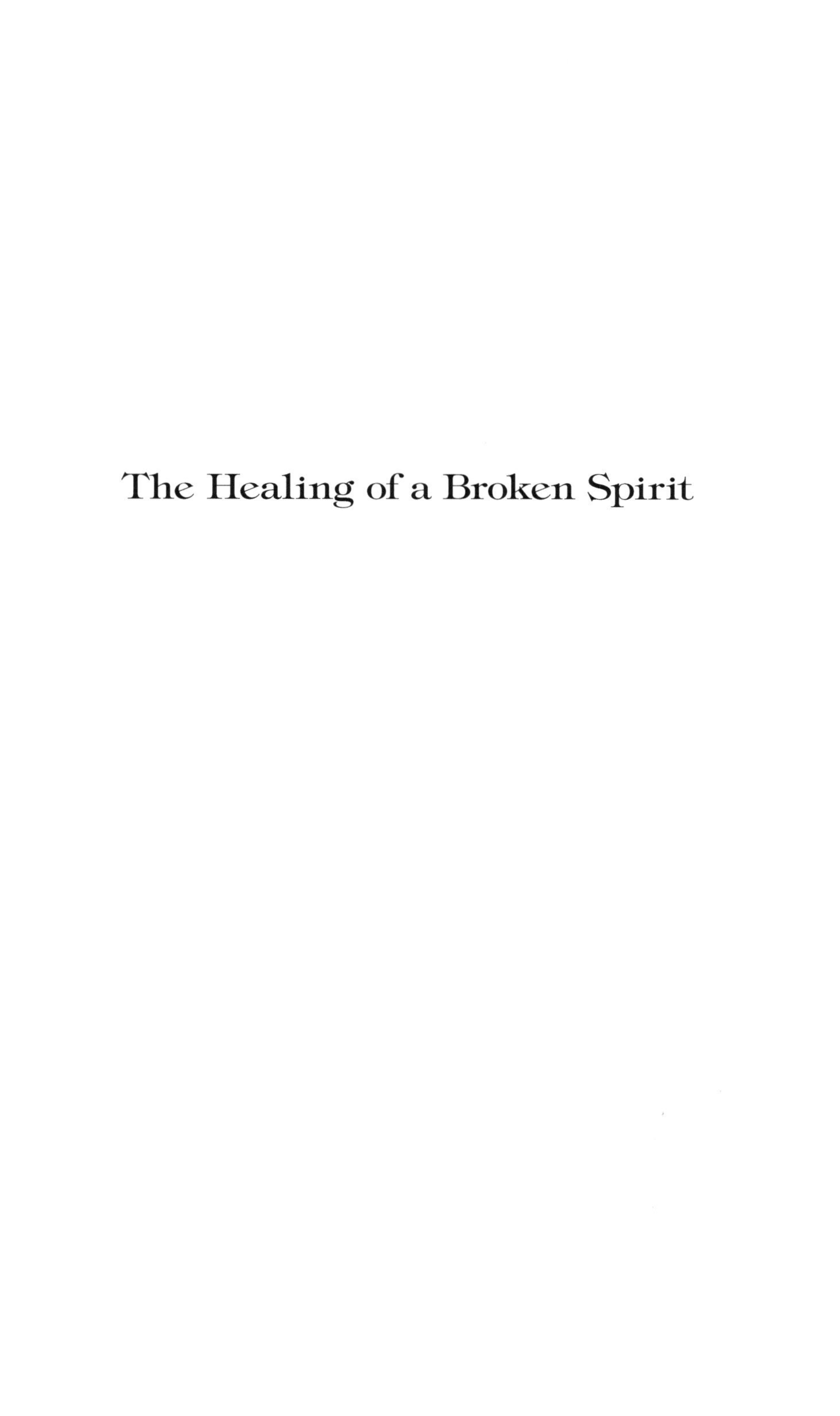

The Healing of a Broken Spirit

The Healing of a Broken Spirit

Akua Fayette

iUniverse

THE HEALING OF A BROKEN SPIRIT

iUniverse books may be ordered through booksellers or by contacting:

iUniverse
1663 Liberty Drive
Bloomington, IN 47403
www.iuniverse.com
1-800-Authors (1-800-288-4677)

ISBN: 978-1-4917-7219-5 (sc)
ISBN: 978-1-4917-7221-8 (hc)
ISBN: 978-1-4917-7220-1 (e)

Library of Congress Control Number: 2015913349

Print information available on the last page.

iUniverse rev. date: 09/03/2015

About the Cover

Highlighted on the cover is the first painting I ever painted for myself. I was inspired after emerging from a "valley moment," a low point in my life, and parts of my vision were based on home, relationships, wisdom, and the influence of women in my life. The purple at the bottom was not planned; it just happened. And now I know why.

Upon visiting a spiritual leader for the fourth time after this book was finished, I needed some insight on what my next move would be. I had gotten there late in the morning, too late to sign up to see the leader privately. He made three appearances before the seated crowd and the many that were standing. He painted a picture with his storytelling that gave me the image for this book on mothers and how they nurture their babies: a bleeding heart wrapped in a blanket, being prepared for the "healing of a broken spirit." When he stated the title of this book, I had received my answer.

Purpose of Intent of Non-Exposure

This publication is written from the eyes and the heart of the writer. This is part of my life journey and my story, leaving out many names and most places to protect the people who are still alive. I have no desire to cause harm or embarrassment to anyone or any organization, but the truth must be told, and no one escapes truth. My family and I have not escaped it either.

There is no hate for or anger at any of my past situations. The healing process of my journey has erased the feelings of being victimized or penalized for past events, which can be labeled mistakes, unjust laws, or tragedy.

In the same way, any pain that may result from my disclosure has not been done with the intent to cause discomfort or to get even. In fact, many of the details have been left out in certain cases. I understand and believe in the power of words and want my words to help to reveal, but also to heal!

This book is written with love and the intention of proving that the truth can set you free, just as I am freed by the revelations of my own disclosures. I too have had to go through the pain of learning certain truths that have shed light on my childhood questions. This book will reveal how children process inner feelings and are sometimes burdened by them, even in our innocence of the situations that we have no control over.

To provide an understanding of how the spirit can be broken during one's lifetime—and for some cultures, like the African American (AA)—it is a different playing field, yet the game must go on. And therefore, as AAs, we must go back to the very roots of our existence and get what belongs to us—our *whole* spirits, the blessing of being free in mind and body, and knowing the difference between how and where we survive and how and where we thrive!

This book is written with the names of places, locations, and people changed in most cases, to protect those who may prefer privacy.

This Book Is Dedicated

To all who crossed my path, each adding *color* to my life and helping to make my journey look like …

Jacob's coat
feeling like I have arrived
where I belong
without the one thing my loving mother never told me …

Finding the truth has set me free. This truth stirred my soul and made me know my daddy really loved me despite the situation.

My mother gave me a jumping pad like none other, but she also delivered me to the place that is *now* a launching pad.

I owe my uniqueness and strength to her and my talents to her sister, my aunt, whom she loved dearly, and her mother, Grandmother Pearl, the poet and songwriter.

Special thanks to Mr. Randle, who was like a father and still is.

Contents

Introduction

Writing has been part of the journey that I have been waiting for, but not quite like this. I never thought that I would be like the people I have watched on *Oprah* spilling their family histories in public (or even as Oprah herself, putting her life story in full view), although I do respect people who stand up to their truths. But I will bring the proverbial *laundry* out of the closet of my family's life. This has been one way others have been able to stand up, to know they were not alone, and I have always known that something was not being brought out in my family either.

I've been told that I have an investigative nature, and I guess it started at an early age. Being the tenth child really contributed to my gaining some skills. It also made me curious about the world around me and my older siblings, who ranged from five to nineteen when I was born. They seemed big compared to me by the time I could be outside on my own. Times were different then; there really was a village concept. Everyone basically looked out for one another's children.

By the time I was three or four, I was already engaged in conversations, asking questions, wondering about this *big mystery* in the sky called *God* or Jesus. I was drawn in by the beautiful, fluffy white clouds and their shapes hovering over me, always there and never the same. Each time, I tried to identify what the shapes meant to me.

I was also trying to get past other questions too—like why my relationship with my father was so strange. I could not say what it was that felt different … but by the time I was eight, I was more aware something was not the way it should be.

Once married and having a family of my own, I faced other challenges. I'd wanted to have children right away. The first prayer answered was a strong and intelligent boy. He literally came into this world spinning out in the air like a football. A friend was there, as the midwife had not made it—I only had three labor pains before he was born, tiny but alert.

I became pregnant the second time much sooner than I'd planned. The birth of my second child was harder. I became immobile, paralyzed, and I was faced with death or at the least the risk of being an invalid at the age of twenty-one. Just as witnessing my father's death prompted spiritual insights, this near-death experience prompted the greatest spiritual advancement thus far in my life. It taught me where I could find God—as if he were lost! I *found* God inside, and that brought me to a miraculous healing from what had been severe loss of movement and excruciating pain from anyone's touch. This second birth experience turned out to be a blessing in many ways—for the beautiful, sensitive, intelligent baby girl that came to us and also for the lessons I learned, including humility. I could never pass by a person in a wheelchair after that and not feel compassion. I understood the journey of being physically challenged.

Thirty years later, this experience inspired me to paint a picture and write a poem, both named "The Angel behind the Chair," about the awesome responsibility of those who push and guide those of us in wheelchairs; our very lives are in their hands as they maneuver us around, sometimes in very dangerous situations. I see it as an act of love, and I love helping people in wheelchairs even to this day. I see it as a blessing to open a door or guide them to safety.

Once back on my feet, my own faith was challenged: Would I ever be able to have another child? About four years later, I succeeded in getting pregnant. Stating that God doesn't *half heal*, I proved that theory to be right for me. I even had the third baby naturally and at home, as I had the first and second. I was determined—and willing—to go the whole mile with my faith.

This was one of the best challenges to my faith, and it paid off—with a beautiful, intelligent, sweet, loving, old spirit, my youngest child.

She is part of the reason I found the answer to my lifelong question: *Why did Mama love Daddy so much?* She is the one who followed up on the invitation that led me to the spiritual leader who gave me not only the answer to the question but the title of this book. The rest will be history.

Both daughters brought God into my life in different ways; as they are as different as day and night, I teasingly call them Dusk and Dawn.

In 1983, the year that brought two great losses upon my family—the death of my dear mother and the loss of my husband's job—I developed my "broom theory." The oil industry had gone downhill in Texas, and many oil workers (like my husband) lost their jobs, their homes, and their families through divorces and breakups as the economic needle went downward. I had no choice but to call up the energy of "I can make it for myself." This was what I called my Broom Theory, the idea that I could always pick up a broom and sweep myself out of trouble. I had my own little decorating and wallpaper business and invited my husband to join forces with me. He did, and our home-based business prospered for twelve years.

And then I hit another life-changing snag. I felt that I was out of order, out of balance, and could not define my real purpose. I realized when I saw a black man walking down the street of our community, the ink on the deeds of the houses still said something to the effect, "This house cannot be sold to a nonwhite." Things had changed, with integration and money, we were able to buy, but seeing my reactions to him (the strange black man) helped me change my life's direction, once again. Now I was feeling an urgency to live in a community that I could identify with and be of another type of service. I had no idea where this was going to take me.

We found a way to buy a house, putting the broom theory back into force. We raised the money methodically, one job and project at a time. We put in a bid, won the bid, and got it very cheap, in the old neighborhood where we once had rented as some of the first blacks to integrate it. It now lay wasted, with many houses on many streets looking as if there had been a war—doors, windows, and anything metal had been removed. I was one of those who had followed the "white flight," being in neighborhoods where I did not have to worry about getting involved. And here I was now, turning around and going back to what had become a battle zone.

Now I wanted to know who would do the work. The answer was me and my family. This led me into community activism, which led me into another community of support for how to work and save a community!

I first tried working with the police department, until a sting operation proved that "leaks" were blocking our progress. That was when I decided I would not try to stop or control drug dealers—I wanted to get to the minds and hearts of the women and children, to *prevent* drug users as well as the poverty that was brought on by lack of cultural pride, ethics, education, and wisdom.

Once it had been established that there were a few bad policemen on the take, and someone had made threatening remarks about me being an easy target while working in my yard or at some community cleanup action I might be working on, I knew I had to get help.

I had never attended a civic-club meeting in the suburbs or upper-class communities where I'd lived—*they* (white people) handled that. *We* (black people) just kept our own property well managed. Now I felt forced by necessity to start a "civic club" of my own.

I knocked on door after door and set up plans to protect the elderly who were afraid to call the police. They could call me, and I would report the activity.

I wanted to help teach children to understand prejudice and racism, but not to fear people or judge others by what was on the outside. So I used geese as my characters—one from the past, one from the present, and one from the future—in a series of storybooks called *Goose Sense.* My art and work has been aired on TV, and I have won awards for my activism. My desire is to make a difference, to show love and remove hate, to develop our lives by beautifying our dwelling places, to *think positive* and spread hope. We can do so much.

My purpose began to take shape as I saw injustice and the abuse of children. I began to paint and use it symbolically to help alert black people that we have power to help ourselves, to take care of our children, to keep them safe. I set another example with symbolic art, showing that women could unite and make a difference, with three paintings:

The Three Sisters, *The Mother*, and *Baby Wrapped in Gold (Children Are Our Greatest Treasure)*.

Being haunted by my childhood questions, I created the poetry CD, *Black Love and a Cup of Coffee Goes a Long Way*. The title and concept came out of my positive association with coffee drinking—even when there was little food, there was always coffee and love from my mother. The CD is available on Amazon.com.

My activism led me to many organizations where we worked for social justice. As a young girl, I did not like to listen to the news or radio talk shows. Then I became a news reporter for public radio. I also became a cohost on a Sunday night public radio show and on two commercial radio talk shows. I was "commissioned" to write this book, and the universe opened up to help me do it.

There are many lessons to learn in my stories, but there is something that leads me to give my intentions to new laws so that justice can prevail in more ways than one. Families are struggling and being torn apart by visible and invisible distractions; love is being lost, and lives are being taken. I have faced some fierce trials while writing this book—trust me, there is a method to the madness we see—and you may find yourself asking for the answer to your life story. It sounds funny, but most of us knew something that we could not explain as children. We do have the ability to change our lives, and it's by the mere reversing of the thought patterns we have used in our minds.

I am laying my life open to help others. I am exposing myself and those I love to help others, and possibly, it will help you, dear reader.

Return to Purple

A spiritual journey led by vibrations of colors …

Nearly fifteen years ago, I became obsessed with the color purple. I incorporated the color into nearly every painting and object I touched. I felt so engrossed with the color that I literally told my friends and family—in a joking way—if they saw me with purple paint, to take it from me!

One thing I realized about purple: it is not for full view on a courtyard wall. It began to have a reverse effect on me as I finally grasped why the sky is blue, the grass is green, and the earth is brown. These are soothing colors, and color does have an effect on our emotional states.

Well, purple is back in my life. And now I know why it has taken me more than fifteen years of continuing on my journey of art and symbolism and the last ten years of radio to know how to use it. I have found out more about who I am and what my journey details, which is exciting. But this time, I will use my purple sparingly—but with pride and in many areas: in my decor, in my wardrobe, and in my garden.

My spouse and I are redoing another house as I write this. I was told by my oldest daughter that I was too old to be buying a house. And she especially advised not to use it for storage—even for the short term! This was good advice. So I decided to use the new space for our retirement dwelling. This house is well planned.

I had already decided to use indigo blue after discovering that I was on point with my destiny to move to a new house and getting it ready for entertaining. The next color I had in mind was purple, and of course, that is my next year's color for personal growth, reaching further into spirituality and sharing what I know. So now we have blue, gold, and purple as the colors that are going into this house. Our thoughts and plans for the purpose of this house will be a place to enjoy family and friends, showing gratitude for where we are and what we plan for our community.

This book, which I abbreviate as *HBS*, might seem unique. And it is—because it is not just about me, my opinions, or my definitions. I have sought out many of the people who have given me a little bit of the "rope to climb out of the basket," and I am grateful and privileged for their contributions.

It would not be my story if it was not done the way my life has been orchestrated. The book was easy to write, a little hard to organize, but the hardest part was that it opened up my mind, my heart, and my spirit to things I had not shared with many. I had not even ever written myself an appropriate bio. The first one I had was written by young lady who was an associate of one of my best clients. The second one was by a radio-host friend and "brother." (It actually brought tears to my eyes.) I was amazed they had taken such notice of my body of work.

Most of my acquaintances do not know the places I have been or some of the people I have met. I have worked for one of the most well-respected architects of Houston, Texas, who designed a great shopping center where two of my associate/friends work. One of these is the first black female judge in the county elected the same time as two other black women running for local office. This architect and his gracious wife taught me about valuable antiques and lights and lamp design in decorating.

A black federal judge I knew—who had a building named in his honor in another state—commissioned me to custom paint light switches for his entire home. I have also exhibited my symbolic art for a Republican black judge in his actual courtroom—the same place a few relatives and friends of mine have had to stand, for different reasons.

Houston Community College-Southwest (HCC-SW)

Thank you … so very much.
Words cannot express the feeling—
Displaying my art from floor to ceiling
In the beautiful gallery you so graciously made available.
For the reception award and the beautiful table,
Your facility was such a great place to display
My art and the warm words that you did say.
Here is a little original token of my thanks so true—
The mini–art especially done just for you.
(A card alone was not enough.)

I have for the last ten years wanted to do a one-woman art show, being that my art expresses with symbolism the same issues that reach across my activism—on race, family, child abuse, sisters' relationships, marriage, community, children's stories of history and culture. Southwest Houston Community College made that possible.

This was the first complete showing of my art from beginning to now. It showed the vast changes in my style from the realism of age twenty-six to the symbolic styles that help heal broken spirits that I started using at age forty-four. My purpose has not changed, but it is moving to a higher level of gratitude and love for humanity in its best form, *love.*

I am grateful, for this contact from my son Ishman, who referred me to HCC.

Special thanks to those who took the time out to attend the event.

A special thanks to my daughter who helped me to set up the exhibit, which was, we were told, one of the best and most beautifully arranged shows they've had—and of course with the most variety, as I included works made of wood, on canvas, objects, and my "Stump People," who were featured in the gallery advertisements.

Special thanks also to David Sincere and Sincere Media for the filming of the SW Houston Community Art Gallery exhibit.

And also to a very special person and friend, Michelle Barnes, who helped open many doors within the community and the HMFA (Houston Museum of Fine Arts) (to my work.

Special Page of Gratitude

To my soulmate, Imhotep, for "allowing" me the privilege to be either a stay-at-home mom or a boardroom mom, and not holding me to either. I have been free to be me and to grow over forty-five years of marriage, and I am not quitting as long as there is air to breathe. Even when my ideas were doubted, you stood by every move. Thanks for that love and support. Thank you also for *renaming* me over twenty years ago.

And to the memory of my beloved mother, whom I adored to the point that I lived most of my life dedicated to making her life one of ease without having to worry about me giving her any more pain and heartache than she had already been through.

I just know the truth will set you free. I am free now, and so is my mother's memory. She is still the greatest mother to me—not the most perfect, yet her love melted "the sad iron curtains of shame."

Acknowledgments

Having written probably over a thousand poems, and painted twice as many or more objects in my life as a poet and symbolic artist, the inspiration to make a difference has given me creativity to write many short stories and self-publish one from my *Goose Sense* series

The experience of publishing my first book, a children's book, was a "spirit-breaking experience," because I wanted a certain kind of person to do it and did not "let go and let God" to direct me. So because the offer was not one I could accept, at the risk of losing all my rights to my work, it has been on the shelf, after having it done professionally. Nonetheless, the content and the intent were and still are inspiring and appreciated. *And* ... it is about to come off that shelf soon!

After thanking God, who has delivered me from so many situations and carried me when I *literally* could not walk, I must give thanks to my soul mate for life, Imhotep, for he has always supported me in a way that has allowed me to fulfill my desires. Even when he did not understand my choices, he supported me. He has been the wind beneath my wings, the cloud over my head, and occasionally the pebble in my shoe, and all of it has made me grow in my search to become a better person for my creative and exciting purpose.

I was told to write this book by a highly spiritual person. I was given the title by him, *The Healing of a Broken Spirit*. I will begin by thanking the glorious spirits, spiritual guides, and the brotherhood who protect and surround me on a daily basis, and the vessel in which they used a special spiritual person to let me know the direction I should take.

Thanks to all the people who have come into my life in the last four years, preparing me for that *special visit* I will speak of in this book. Especially "Martha," a short-term life interaction but a lifelong friend and personal angel sent to bring me peace in my life during one of my biggest challenges.

The news department of the public radio that gave me my first "break" in radio—thanks to Renee. I walked in one day on my own, with no referrals, did an interview and was soon doing special news reports. I was told I was a *natural*. (I must admit that my spouse had been encouraging me to do radio for a long time—he says it was because I talked so much!) It was fun, but then I had the opportunity to *cohost* on a nighttime talk show! Thanks to Dr. OK; he became my "little" brother. And I cannot leave out his wife, who supports him and those who love him (the PTTPP—pepper to the political pot), Mr. C., or dependable and adorable Brother Dean, straight from the university, who then later became a teacher and a father. He was our producer for over five years, and I still say he has *the* voice for radio and is a great young man. I am glad Dr. OK wanted me to stay after joining daytime commercial radio for three months. I created a crossover bridge from one radio show to another.

Thanks to Wayne B. and Ernesto for their well-wishes as I stayed on radio for those three months and did both shows before leaving. Dr. OK's son then became our producer. We celebrated seven years on the show together.

Thanks to *my* son, who supported us many nights on the board and did great advertisement posters for us, as well as my grandson, "Bud."

I am thankful for the lessons I learned at another radio station, where I volunteered and got on-air experience for what commercial radio was about—oh, but I had much to learn. They gave me motivation to move forward.

I am at a loss when I think of the people who stayed the course with me throughout my career of community service and my "art ministry." For that is what it turned out to be for the people who were helped by its positive purpose and mission to enlighten the world about the beauty and the strength of God.

I must list as many as possible, for this is the community and the color added to my life: the opportunity to do TV, radio, interviews, documentaries, presentations, exhibits, speaking engagements, and to receive awards, medals, design contracts, positive vibrations, and also a few critics who lit my fire.

Thankful also to Betty G. and her husband Weldon for making a wonderful, private place available for me to start this book, so I could be alone.

Black Love and a Cup of Coffee ... My son made the gift of that CD cover

Bill Ward of Song dog Records .graciously recorded the CD on short notice.

All you clients who have bought my art and books and poetry—and many became friends—if your name is not here, you are *not* unappreciated, but I have to stop sometime. Maybe ... the next book?

How this Book Came to Be

I had been writing a book inspired by the hard work of a special elder named Mother Dember., who had recently become a widow. I would like to take the opportunity to give praise and thanks for the memory and the beautiful example her late husband, Clarence Dember, set for the community. He was a humble and loving man, willing to give of his time and talent for the good of the community and to be a complement to Mother Dember. (*Mother. Yes,* that is what we call her.) She helped extend his years with good, healthy food and her passion for a good marriage.

Mother D. is from "Up North" and lives now part-time down south and part-time up north. She is known for her many buttons of political and moral messages that she wears on her hat and her clothing. She is fondly called the Button Lady. I was the first artist she gave permission to paint her image, and I love her sign on the back of her shirt, which states, "Racism is an illness—are *you* sick?"

I see the depth in that question, and as an artist, I sometimes place and extra *i* in the word *illness (illiness)*, because the racist cannot be sick alone. What he has is contagious, and guess what? When I allow it to put hate and fear and anger in me, *I am sick too!* Thus *Love* is the answer to this sickness, and we all need a healing … thus our spirits get "broken" in the process … so I have another slogan to bring it out with another light:

Racism is a disease … would YOU *like to be healed?*

—AF

Love is the prescription.

"Do unto others as you would have them do to you" is the format.

Loving your neighbor as you love yourself is your duty.

In other words, *do your duty* and practice what you preach.

I have found that love is the answer to the question *how do we stamp out racial hate, prejudice, and racism?*

I was given the opportunity to experience a reading from a great spiritual person for my sixty-third birthday. I had no plans to turn my world around by getting an answer to the question I had prepared to ask about my childhood.

This question came about due to a discussion between two of my siblings. The discussion disturbed me, as one of my siblings reported back to me what was said, something about my father. I decided that this would be a question I would ask the spiritual leader. The personal side of this brings humor, for I am always able to see humor in nearly every situation at some point or sometime later, and this was no different.

The person who accompanied me had warned me that sometimes those in the great waiting room can hear the outcries from down the hall, especially when someone is crying. Of course, we chuckled, knowing that would not be the case for us, *hardly*. Then my companion informed me she heard someone crying softly, and she thought "Ooh, he got to her," until she realized the person who was weeping softly was me! I was just as surprised at the outburst, but not as much as by the information that would be given later, which not only changed my outlook on my past but also my future. We later laughed at the absurdity of it all. I thought, "Who me, crying?" Another example of God's sense of humor.

Now that some family secrets were out of the bag, *many* questions were automatically answered. I had even written poetry as a child regarding these questions concerning my mother's love and loyalty to my father despite his issues that caused us to go without and move from pillar to post.

I also began to realize why certain people began to show up in my life.

Upon the second visit to this great spiritual leader, I found him to be accurate in his predictions in my life. He knew things that no one could know unless connected to a greater power—and as we are taught that God knows all we do, I guess we must believe "spirits," "angels," or "guides" might be with us and can report on what is and what will be.

I have often wondered, as we read Bible stories, why some of these miracles and great future readings—prophecies—aren't as prevalent today. Well, I have found life opens up its knowledge when we get out of the *box of control*. I truly believe Jesus when the Bible quotes him saying, "You can do greater things than me," if we follow and obey God's way. There are people who dedicate their lives to God and are in tune with the spirit world.

I will reveal this spiritual leader in the chapter that tells of my visit and his predictions. He counsels with presidents, great entertainers, high government authorities, and most of all, he talks to about a hundred people a day—individuals and groups—everyday people from all walks of life.

I had been writing feverishly about love and peace and felt the title for my book, inspired by Mother D., would be about love. But he pointed to my heart and said, "You have a book inside you … Here is the title … *The Healing of a Broken Spirit*."

He interrupted me as I was about to explain the book I was writing … "This is the title," he said once again. He told me more about what would happen with this book and its destiny. Upon finishing this book, I will make a separate note about his prophecy, but for now, I will keep it unknown, for it outweighs anything that I would have thought would happen. The book you have has parts of my life that I would never have revealed—without the divine purpose, that is, to heal and help others who find or have found themselves in my situations. And please, be careful not to judge, because those helped could be and will be some of you who are reading this book. We are so connected and share the common threads of human failure that God uses as stepping stones. And if we open our hearts, our minds, and our spirits, you will allow them to become launching pads!

There are a few things that I have not shared with some of the closet people I know and love, and yet there have been times I have shared very painful experiences, such as my father's death, with a stranger. To help someone, like a child going through the death of a loved one, for example, I have shared most of the important and life-changing things I have faced, to help someone know that they can do more than survive—they can thrive and excel!

I knew that one day my story needed to be told, to be handed down to my grandchildren and generations to come. I did not know what

I learned at sixty-three would be a part of my story, that I would be sharing the family pride we children had as one family.

I Want Young Artists to Know That ...

Art is a beautiful thing and everything is art.

—AF

Everything created and designed started with a thought. God's creations: the soft glow of the moon, the warmth of the sun, the shade of the trees, the stillness of a mountain, and the movement of air. Delight in the great bodies of water, gray, green, blue, and white ... yes, it is all art. We are the very work of God's art ourselves.

I beg to differ with people who say they have no art ability. We all have certain abilities; we are from the greatest artist ever, the Creator Divine of the Universe. I use art in my activism. If a picture can speak a thousand words, and I have a thousand words to speak and a creative mind to paint ... how much more powerful can that be?

Be Aware When God Is Showing You a *Sign*

As a little girl I wanted to be a ballerina. I could stand on my toes. I had strong legs, but the lack of money did not make me feel hindered, it was the blackness of my culture that made me feel that it could not be. I had never seen a black ballerina, but then, I had not seen a black angel either, and that would later be of importance to my art.

I never felt poor. I guess it was about the frame of mind, and poor meant a mind-set to me. My ability to measure wealth at an early age showed me it was more than material value. Wealth was your *integrity*. It was having a word that people could trust. As a teenager, my selection of a young man was based on his politeness, his intelligence, and his moral values. I was not wowed by cars and money.

I entered an essay contest when I was young, which was open for the first time to blacks, and I won. That year, also for the first time, they did not make any placement of first, second, or third place. We (two white children and myself) were on channel 13, my first TV appearance! The essay was entitled "Respect the Law and It Will Respect You!" Little did I know that was a "sign"—not only for more TV spots in my future but that the true laws of the universe *will* respect you if you respect them; with man, there is still much injustice.

The second thing I remember wanting to be was a designer. I loved drawing clothes and decorating. I remember my mother helping me build a huge playhouse, big enough for me to stand in and decorate. I always helped Mother choose colors and change the furniture around the room in our real house.

The third thing was my desire to design homes—I would dream plans and buy magazines about homes—an architect. I did enjoy the opportunity to make changes in the design of homes in our business, when we painted, wallpapered, and did some structural changes to them. These skills were taught to my husband and me by the late Mr. Ross, the architect in Houston who designed the great shopping center I described earlier. Later, I will share how we came to work for such a unique and kind couple as he and his wife.

I did not start my art or my storytelling until I was in my early forties, but it came fast. About 1999, I was selected by PBS to have an interview on my work as an artist, activist, author, and a storyteller. These interviews typically featured three people. The two persons who were featured with me were a black ballerina and a black male architect! How interesting is that? I took them as signs. These are the sorts of subtle things that are laid in our paths that we sometimes pay no attention to.

The story of my multifaceted life includes my work in the community and then the crises of my loved ones, when my oldest daughter was challenged with cancer and my oldest brother was challenged with an emergency operation on his colon. All that came out in the interview.

The PBS special won an Emmy award for its host, Doris Childress, and commissions for my art and myself in the silent auction for the Deep in the Heart of Houston Gala, which was commissioned by Mayor Lee P. Brown. And it took my art internationally and me for a three-week stay at Walt Disney Studios, another out-of-nowhere blessing that I received.

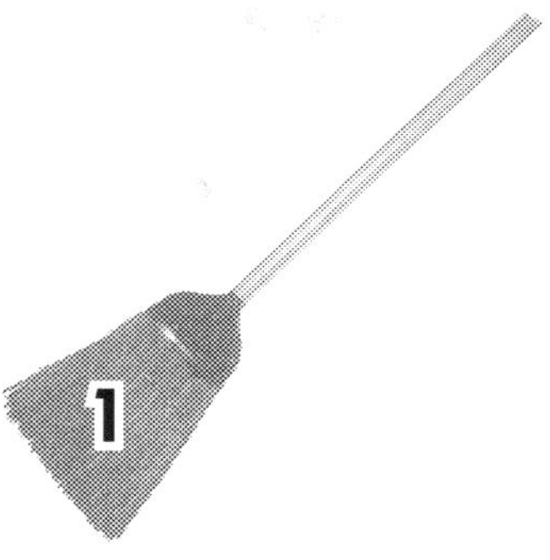

Healing ... of a Broken Spirit

Looking back on my life it was destiny for me to understand *brokenness,* as I was born to a family with a unique brokenness—a mother who lost her mother at the age of thirteen. My maternal grandmother died suddenly while pregnant with twins, who died also, leaving my mother without a parent. But she did have two older brothers and several sisters and the one sister we came to know as "Teen," who loved her dearly. My mother's brothers would soon forget family ties. That was another kind of brokenness that has been passed down into the family.

My father was born under one name but lived under another name, which we all ten children carried. Two girls died, one at three months, the other at nearly two years old, both tragically—one through a doctor's error in giving her an overdose of medication, and the other drowned.

My father did not have any formal training, as he was raised under the burden of an abusive stepfather and a mother who would sometimes sacrifice herself by throwing her body upon his to take the hits of the strap aimed at him from her "husband," his stepdad.

As a young person, I can remember my siblings having the kind of conversations like "What if our parents had been fully educated? How great they might have been."

My father masked not being able to read with the ability to do many other things quite well—possibly, if it had not been for the drinking, which would turn our world upside down, there may have been a different outcome.

Therefore, I lived in a world of intelligent people who had little formal training. My mother loved her children, even though her way of expressing it was *different*. She was a serious, kind, and soft woman who oozed poise, dignity, respect—and that sometimes annoying *privacy*.

The hugging, kissing kind of love was not the way she expressed it to us, but it was the "show me what you are working with" kind of love—the kind that I so relate to and the kind that I exhibit. I expressed that kind of love in a poem named "Different Ways to Love."

She was kind but no-nonsense, giving, compassionate, and attentive to our personal needs and pains. I have been learning more how to show my love with the hugs and the kisses.

Being the last child, I saw much drama among the older brothers and sisters. In many ways, we were the norm, and in some ways, we were the exception, as my mother was educated with about a fourth-grade education, but she was very intelligent. She read and kept abreast of current events and world news. She knew how to save money and had a deep feeling of personal pride in her appearance and her children. We were taught to not leave the house looking just any kind of way, and even if we only had bread to eat, to walk as if we had had a three-course meal. I was an aunt by the time I became two and a half years old.

I was able to appreciate the positive and the negative of any situation, even as a child. That was my special gift of survival. This book was *commissioned* for me to write by someone that is so respected he was invited to visit with Oprah a number of times (though he refused because he wanted to be able to serve the "little people." He knew that Oprah's Midas touch would make him too popular.). He is someone who has counseled presidents and mayors. Ironically, one of the mayors was the only mayor I ever presented a piece of my original art to, in his honor, and President Obama is the only person I personally worked for in a campaign and the only president that I have had personally shake my hand. I also had the privilege of meeting one of Oprah's employees—at Walt Disney Studios. The employee had plans to connect me with Oprah, but the time was not right, I thought, for me, as my oldest daughter had just been diagnosed with lymphoma cancer. Family comes first, when it comes to those life-and-death situations. I'm thankful that God is a divine healer. My daughter is a survivor and a strong-spirited person.

I am grateful for my journey—sometimes hard and sometimes easy, but it is all good and has brought me this far. So as you read about my journey, remember I am not trying to expose anyone personally, especially my siblings. I will let them tell their own stories, for as I have found out, we all see things in different lights; that's why it is important to tell your own. I felt it important to get the approval of all my siblings to expose some truths that would be painful to my parents if they were alive, and the one I have not asked is the one who drove me to find the answer to my lifelong riddle: Why did Mama love Daddy so?

I hope you will also understand even more so … how the truth can set you free!

Dog Is One of *Woman's* Best Friends

I ended this edition of *The Healing of a Broken Spirit I,* as I started it: alone with my little dog, Miracle, and it has been a miracle! She has stayed the course with me, by my side, as I write quietly, never complaining, giving me much love. She was about three months old when I started on day-one with the title; she is now two years old—not too much bigger and so very much as sweet.

Miracle the serious look as the IPad rest on her

How someone with my background could aspire to write such a book, some may wonder, but the last twenty-five-plus years of my life have been the best university I could have attended. I did go back to college for a course in African history, a wonderful class. I met some great people. The course was given by the Taseti Historical Society. I did finish the course, and what I learned gave me a great foundation of the beauty and knowledge that we as a people have given to this world.

I have been surrounded and befriended by people of all cultures, genders, faith, and occupations—as one might say, from the outhouse to the White House—and I have literally had my hand shaken by the candidate Barack Obama, simply because I gave up my position in line to help the other people in line, which was so long for security reasons—by visiting them to make them feel comfortable instead of going inside and getting up front with the media. Of course, I was disappointed at first that I had lost my place up in the front, but once inside, I was united with people trying to get to the president-to-be, and he made the effort to reach out and touch my hand. That was a gift of doing the right or the kind thing: *you won't be forgotten.* Besides, I did enjoy talking to the weary people in line waiting for security to check them out.

I was surprised as I began to thank the organizations, schools, universities, businesses, and social media that have given this Fifth Ward … colored, Negro, black, African … child of God the opportunity to reach the heights that she still had time to soar!

Age is a number, but life is energy, hope, faith, boldness. One of my daughters said over a year ago, "Mom, you and Dad are too old to be buying a house, much less remodeling it." Now, I sit in that house that I've almost finished as I write. Having to do this book and redesign this house in the *'hood*, has been a blessing. This is a place of peace, calm, and beauty of cultures. And yes, I am not through yet, because ….

It's really not over until the Black Lady quits *singing!*

—AF

Researching from Within

The book is finished, and I am just now looking online and researching what information and images are available on broken spirits and healing. One might ask, why didn't you research before you started? Because I was told to *feel* the story that I had to write inside of me, and like my art and my poetry, it was all inside of me. I recall Gary Zukav saying he read no book and was not influenced by anyone while writing *The Seat of the Soul*. It made me feel better about many of my life choices of seldom reading others' poetry and not wanting a famous art teacher, just to say I studied under "Such and Such." I wanted the "raw me."

It's funny, when I took about eight lessons from a neighbor who was an excellent painter, a copy artist (she painted what she saw, and imitated it well), I found I could do that also. So the first three paintings that I did looked amazing for a beginner—so much, she refused to teach me anymore! I was glad to put my paints away for over twenty years, until I came to a community art project where I met young artists. Once again, the spark of art inside me came out, but this time it was from me! I would paint with no visuals and with the purpose of lifting black women in our quest for beauty. We are as God has created us.

My first project was to tackle the hair issue, and the title was *What's a Sister to Do?* This drawing was of a black woman with about ten styles coming from her head, with a puzzled look. My art then went to painting on tiles left over from a tile job we had donated to a project for a meeting place for Sisters in Positive Progress. Each tile had a different hairstyle and different shades of color.

But I wasn't pleased with the outcome, for the paintings to me were not as good as the polished young artists I was surrounded by. What I noticed was that my intent, my love, my desire, and my authenticity of hope for the message of acceptance of us all, of each other, *was* captured. I hung the painted tiles around the "row house" (a style of building, dating back to African design, the same style of house I grew up in, and the only home we ever owned). I would walk into the shop and be embarrassed by my attempt to symbolize my feelings of the beauty of our differences as black women, But something great happened: women loved the art and started buying them off the wall, though they were not for sale. I had to remove the rest as to preserve my first attempt in symbolic art messages for positive images.

The next piece was *Baby Wrapped in Gold (Children Are Our Greatest Treasures).* I was walking into the shop one morning with an 11 x 17 sheet of paper, and a middle-aged white woman stopped me and asked, "How much do you want for that painting?"

It was an original, but I was new to this portion of the art business and did not have a clue what to charge. But being a business person who painted houses, wallpapered, and so forth, I came up with a price—sixty-five dollars, to be exact. She did not blink an eye; she went to her car and handed me cash. I was shocked that my art could sell so easily! At least I still have the print I made from it! I would love to see her today and say, "You gave me my start in believing people wanted my art … thanks."

Then I was told that only white people would buy my art, because black people did not appreciate black art. I was told I would starve waiting for art to pay for food. I knew words were powerful, and I, at forty-two, and new to the "art world" was moving faster than some of my peers who had been in the art world over twenty years, were way ahead of me, and had not been invited to the places to exhibit that were inviting me, with only four months "under my belt."

I know more now. While putting this book together, I was on-purpose; my art was healing to many because it sent out a positive message. One time, I was commissioned to paint a "black" witch by a potential client—I refused, because it was against my focus on positive images. Yet I use the blackest paint, wanting to show that black has positive attributes, and so do black people. I will go much further in detail about my art experiences at Walt Disney Studios, greeting thousands of people, and the results, as well as my discovery of how much racism makes us victims and sick participants in our own destruction.

My art paid for more than food; it paid for me to give of my time and my service to the community without being beholden to anyone. Anybody who "made" me could "break" me, but instead, the community supported me. Many great black sisters and some white sisters and men have bought my work, and I thank them all. Many have become friends.

The one thing I would like to say: when I started selling my art, women would give me their IDs with their checks. I realized that my art only drew a certain quality of people, and they were honest about wanting my work. I knew an ID would not make a check not bounce, right? So I would say, "I don't need your ID; I just need your phone number. If anything goes wrong, I will give you a call." It was true, and I've never had a bad check in twenty-plus years, and the one that did fail came from a business person who was in the shop with cash the next morning.

God blessed my art, so why should I get a famous artist to front as my teacher and give me an "advantage" in the world of who's who? I had the greatest teacher within, and as long as the message I sent was part of my purpose, it would go well. So as this book was finished, I looked up a broken spirit on the Internet, and was not surprised that what I have been through and how I healed is listed as "How to Heal a Broken Spirit," and so I am placing it in the book, as it is licensed for use to help others. I do believe part of my purpose is to give hope to the "little people," those who lack financial resources, family security, formal education, and so forth. Hope that you can survive the broken spirts in your life. God, which brings Love, is the answer; sometimes it only takes something as simple as *letting go and letting God,* picking up your "broom" … and doing your duty!

What is this broom? My broom has been many things: my pen and paper, my paint brush—both types, the working type and the fine-art type—my character, my words, my deeds, my ability to make lemons into not only lemonade but cookies pies, sauce, and candy. Knowing it is sour, but it can bring the best result for my health, so I have learned to enjoy even the raw lemon juice in life … and a little cool water helps it go a long way.

The Broom Theory Comes into Practice

Over forty years ago, I decided to leave college and go to a very *southern* state, where my soul mate awaited, to marry me.

Due to religious teaching and the prejudiced times in which we lived, the church I attended, The World Wide Church of God had over a million members worldwide and three college campuses (African American youth were not encouraged to go to school beyond high school and were not allowed to attend the university that was owned by the church unless they were married. This was intended to stop integrated dating within the church, but the greater problem was that we were also taught not to date outside of the church … so being in a white-dominated church as a black teenager was a challenge. Though it was a corrupt system, whatever I set my mind to do I always tried to follow through on. That is what I did when I accepted, at the age of ten (I was given the opportunity to accept or not) to give up a mainline Christian church to join a more "stick-to-the-Bible version." We kept all the holy days mentioned in Leviticus, and we followed the Hebrew diet of no pork, so I was what one would call a Christian/Jew or Hebrew Israelite, although the church said we were nondenominational.

But remember, I am African American, so in 1960, I was definitely living in a black community. Nonetheless, I was able to survive, because I had learned early that we *teach* people how to treat us by how we treat ourselves and what we allow them to get away with toward us. I was in the top 5 percent of my class, despite the disadvantages of my lifestyle, which required me to bow out of many activities, along with being the tenth child of a poor widow (my father also died when I was ten).

Like so many young girls, my greatest dream was to be a great designer and decorator and to marry the man of my dreams—who was to have my father's best attributes and *not* his worst. At an early age, I could dissect character and extract good from bad and not hate the person even if they did wrong. So my father ended up being my greatest teacher in what to look for and what not to look for in a husband. I have a poem about this entitled "Why Did Mama Love Daddy So?" The poem describes my father's lesson in "What is and what isn't a good man?"

I first saw my husband-to-be for only a few minutes one year; I was sixteen. The next year, we met in East Texas for our church's annual "Feast" holiday, which would last eight days. (Yes, I would be out of school with a religious permit for a total of about thirteen to fifteen days a year for various holy days.) I was seventeen now, and we did volunteer work in Church College's kitchen, and we begin to talk a little the last day of the Feast. He asked for my address and phone number.

About ten months went by, and I was in college and doing well when he asked me to go to the church dance with him. I hesitated to say yes, since it had taken him so long to write! Then I found out he had lost his mother just before he graduated that past year and he had a younger brother to whom he was responsible—life had been quite full of unexpected responsibilities. Anyway, by now my mother was already concerned, because she felt, at eighteen, if I didn't meet someone I wanted to date *in* the church, I would end up dating someone *outside* it. So because of my mother, whom I respected and loved, I said yes to his invitation.

Mother could not go that year, so I lived with an eighty-year-old woman named Ms. Powell. We camped on the campus of the university with about ten thousand other members from around the world! All the black people who had to come to Texas were all camping in one spot—mainly to keep us segregated from the whites and together "in one area." The best part of this racist arrangement turned out to be a great event for the youth. We had the opportunity to meet black teenagers from all over the United States, so meeting young men and women from New York, Chicago, Georgia, Washington, Arizona, L.A., and other places was exciting, but my prayers and my insights led me to the dark-skinned handsome young black man, Imhotep, with the million-dollar smile. Many of the young people were rebellious toward the rules of the church, especially those from up north. I liked young men who were nice, smart, and not lazy … Imhotep was a godsend.

We were together every day of the Feast; we went to all the services, and ate out together in the evening one very cold night. He gave me and Ms. Powell the heater that he and his brother shared in their tent, to keep us warm in our tent. Yep, he was the one. His brother was upset at him, though, for giving the heater to some "girl." The campsite was huge, and of course, if there were forty streets, the blacks were on the last ones, with no electrical outlets for trailers and no paved streets.

On the last day of the Feast, Imhotep gave me my first kiss, which was on the cheek, and put his class ring on a chain around my neck. I learned later from his sister that he loved that ring so much, they knew this had to be special.

About six weeks later, I got my usual Sunday phone call. He would go over to Mr. Bee's house, the local black minister in the church, who lived a few streets from his sister, and he would call me and later pay Mr. Bee for the long-distant calls (things have really changed since the cell phone, for the good and the bad). I would be in the bathtub, bathing as usual, because this was the only real *private* place we could talk. Now that I think about it, we had many conversations with me naked on the phone! Thank goodness phones had no vision back then! He asked me on October 11, 1967, if I would marry him. My answer was yes. Three months later, I was being seen off by my family and a few friends in the church on a "midday train to the Deep South."

We were in the middle of history, with race riots and marching all over the south, so you can imagine how fearful some people were for me to go to *the Deep South,* especially by myself.

I lived with his oldest sister, and he had already rented a small, cute house two doors down from her. This would be our first house when we got married.

Two months after I arrived, Martin Luther King was assassinated, and two months after that, Bobby Kennedy. There was also personal grief: my brother's girlfriend had been murdered, and my mother was left to take care of their nine-month-old son.

Actually, my mother and my nine-month-old nephew—we called him PD (people had strange nicknames back in the day for children)—were the only blood relatives to attend my wedding. But I was excited, because my mother was the most important person to me. Imhotep sent the money for her to come down to be there for me.

After living away from Texas for about four months, my new husband announced that we would be moving back to Texas so I could spend my mother's last years with her, being that he loved her too and knew what the loss of a mother was about. He wanted me to enjoy whatever time my mother had left with her. (You can understand why I loved this young man so much.)

We lit out like the black Beverly Hillbillies, with an old trailer that he had rebuilt to hold our new bedroom suite and personal things. We sold and gave away the bulk of our furniture to make the move.

I should have gone back to college, but the church was strong on family and the idea that time was short. In other words, if you don't have your family now, things were going to get so bad—wars and rumor of wars—that many would not have the chance to have families. So I started out wanting to get pregnant after "five long months" of having fun, but then I was trying to decide to go to work. I applied for a job in the art department of a well-known department store in downtown Houston.

I landed the job but failed the health exam. This is what the management told me: they could not hire a pregnant woman. My, how times have changed! The news made me deliriously happy. When my husband came home and saw me looking faint on the couch, he asked, "What's wrong?" I blurted out the name of the department store, and said, "They told me I am going to have a baby!"

I had asked my family and church members to pray that I could get pregnant. And I did! And then I gave birth to my firstborn. But I guess I forgot to tell them to stop praying, because three months later, I was pregnant again! We say she was planned but not planned to come so soon, so we dubbed her our "love child."

With that second birth came a near-death experience that led me to a new faith in being determined to go to God for my own needs. And it worked. I was healed and back on my feet eventually. I then decided to prove that the Creator doesn't half heal, and my having the third baby proved the power of prayer and belief in one's inner ability to engage the secret of healing thyself.

In describing the broom theory, some may think it comes from the ritual of *jumping over the broom,* a tradition in African American marriages going back to when they could not legally marry, as they were the white man's property. But no, I was not aware of that practice when we married in 1968.

There were many people concerned about my choosing to be a stay-at-home mother to raise my children. The question would go like this:

> What will you do if your husband gets sick or leaves you to provide for yourself and your children?

I gave them my broom theory, which went like this:

Life has a way of taking care of us if we believe that we will be provided for, because we all have gifts of some kind, abilities that we must apply in order to survive. By taking a broom and tying a bow around it, I could knock on ten or more doors a day and offer to sweep driveways at ten dollars each, and with that, I could survive.

That was an outlandish thing to say, but it showed my faith in what I chose to do and my belief in honest work having no "low levels." Now, I would not want to do that for a living, but it would be honest work.

Broom Theory 1: From Disaster to Divine Intervention

My broom theory went into action twice during my marriage. After the second baby was born, my husband was in an accident on his job. A pallet of two-by-fours fell about eight feet down onto his back, and he was unable to work. Upon taking him back and forth to the doctor and trying to park free, I would park at the hotel across from his doctor's office. In order not to lie about why I was parking in their parking lot, I went inside and applied for a job as a maid. This would be my excuse for parking there, in case anyone asked, not thinking they would be calling me the next day to work!

Well, they did, and I thought about our situation—so why not take the job cleaning rooms? I could do that and help out. Since my husband was home anyway, he could keep the children. That was our first experience with "job-role change." We both appreciated each other's roles after that experience. I came home wanting peace and quiet, and he wanted to talk after being home with the babies.

The one great thing that came out of that low-wage, honest-job experience was that I gave it my all, treated it as I would any job worth doing: with dignity and gusto. That two-month job then led to an opportunity to work for one of the leading architects of Houston. His wife and he were living at the Motor Inn while they waited for their home in the South West area to be ready to move into. She admired the way I handled myself and the excellent way I cleaned and the service that I gave all the guests.

This broom experience led to the building of the second broom experience.

Her husband came to our home in the south of downtown. We were part of the first group of African Americans to move into the area, and it was quite lovely. Our home, little in comparison to theirs, had charm, and he could see our handiwork in the way my husband and I recessed the mirrors in the walls, recessed the dish cabinets, flocked wallpaper, and so on. He saw an opportunity to take a person with potential and train him to his advantage, and he did. He showed my husband how to read the blueprints of buildings, and the rest is history. Imhotep did an outstanding job in remodeling the architect's home—he converted the front porch into a beautiful entry, open with a view.

Thirteen years later, my second broom-theory experience took place. My mother unexpectedly died, and life took a new a turn during the recession of the oil industry in the early eighties. My husband had gotten his masters in metallurgy and was the first black welder in Texas to be in the Local Pipefitters Union. The company he had been with for eight years had gone bankrupt, and many—the majority, still 98 percent white—lost their jobs, homes, vehicles, and marriages.

We had recently moved into a subdivision known as the Cotton Stocking of Rich Land, a countryside upper-middle-income white neighborhood in Flower Village, a suburb of Houston.

I used to drive through and look at the pecan trees form an arch over the streets like a giant green umbrella. The big old houses sat on half-acre or more lots, with more pecan trees throughout the backyards. We decided on this neighborhood, because we wanted a safe place, with space, and we were adjusted to white people by being brought up in a white church, so we knew we would not have to be bothered with them and they would not be bothered with us. We could raise our children in peace. Now, with my mother's death, we had no employment, except for my small business in wallpaper hanging, painting, and a weekend antique shop and design service.

Broom Theory 2: Partnership and Propulsion

My wallpaper business became the next "broom" when my husband joined with me and we expanded it into roofing, refinishing cabinets, room design, and light remodeling. This lasted for twelve years successfully without any need to advertise. It grew by word of mouth through honesty, good work ethic, and our children, who made great receptionists at answering our phone for business.

Then it happened that I saw a black man walking down the street, where black people hardly ever came on foot. When I heard myself asking what was he doing in the community, "something" asked *me* the same question. Hadn't I been asked what was I doing there? My life changed from that moment: I became restless.

I felt like we had been living on a plantation, because we were known all through the neighborhood and trusted by people with keys to their homes and vehicles and with their alarm codes. People would know who we were working for and who was next on the list. They would call and say, "When you finish the Johnsons', I know you have to do Ms. Williams's porch; would you paint my house next? And if there is someone else on the list, we are willing to wait for you to do the job." After a while, we could not work on our own house, because someone would stop by and say, "You can do your work some other time, I need my work done now." We had so much work in the community, we could walk to one job and the next if we had to.

I finally could not stand the view from my front door, remembering how when my brother would be raking our huge lot, police would stop and ask him if he knew who lived in the house and who was he working for. Once I was looking in my own window, and I was asked by a policeman whose house it was. I was surprised by his attitude and tone of voice.

I wanted out, but it wasn't a good time. Houses were not selling; as a matter of fact, houses were being left to destruction in many neighborhoods. We drove through many of these on the south side, and house after house was deserted and being vandalized. I had a brainstorm idea: since we had two children in college and one in junior high, the only way we could get out was to downsize.

The rest is history. We moved back into the area near where we started out as a young married couple and had our first two children by natural childbirth at home. (I had insisted it could be done, even though it wasn't popular then.)

We knew we wanted a corner house. We found one and made the bid. With no money, we set out a plan to acquire so much per week, and it worked with the help of one friend and one out-of-town relative, who gave us that small part we needed to make the difference. We bought our house with cash, for less than $10,000! There is a separate story about how we came up with the bid price, but suffice it to say, it worked.

But I was shocked at the noise level at night—gunfire and loud voices into the night. During the day, the yards throughout were overrun by weeds, and the sidewalks were covered by grass, leaving only pathways from foot traffic.

I started a civic club to fight the issue of drugs, and then ended up going into another area to learn about community activism. It was reported to me that my life was being threatened for becoming a community activist. It take lots of time, and I see why it's rich people who volunteer, because poor people can't afford to be consistent at something without losing financially, and many fall by the wayside due to lack of support and appreciation.

I developed a project called Volunteer 2000 and mapped out a way for the poor and the middle class to give back to the community. But because my husband and I were teaching a group of activists to restore an old house for a meeting place, I could not activate the solution I designed in V 2000, so I gave away my plan to four organizations in the community. None of them even acknowledged my work. One organization (no longer in existence) sent for someone up north to bring in a plan called Clock Dollar. They paid him to come down to give a workshop. I was quite surprised, because the plan was quite similar to mine, but I had given mine away! At the workshop, I presented my ideas to the person in charge, and he was so impressed he told me later that my plan was more thorough and explanatory than his, so I offered him the plan as well. At that point, I learned the lesson I had been taught as a child: *casting pearls before swine.* I promised myself to never do that again.

Broom Theory 3: Art and Beauty, Business and Operational Money

So the broom this time was my ability to serve people and communicate my ideas through the organizations and businesses that I founded, which was, primarily, a women's organization to support women and children, thus benefiting men and the community. Through this, my paintbrush became my broom.

I paid for my expenses: gas, rent, material, and travel to support my volunteer work through my art. I paved a way to provide for many. My work was fueled by my passion for respecting and giving honor to the color *black.*

For ten years, I have passed up the opportunity to sell myself to the highest bidder by painting what the masses wanted, but instead painted my passion and my calling to bring dignity to black people. Having been brought up in a white racist church, my art became a litmus test for racism. White people who bought my work were aware of what they had to work on in this racist society, for there is no 100 percent escape from it. It is embedded in the core of our country's fabric.

I literally prayed for black people to purchase my work as people kept telling me the real money in art was selling to the white community. I felt I had a commission from my ancestors to reach black women, because my art is how I am able to express my love for our beauty and how the beauty on the inside shines to the outside. Because physical beauty is tarnished by the flaws of poor character, like oxidation to metal.

Even today, as I close in on my next birthday, I realize I feel beautiful when my heart is happy, my faith is strong, and I am forgiving of others as I want others to be forgiving of me. My beauty is captured by my character and my love for my sisters as we strive to bring positive and loving relationships to our communities by the way we share information and our ethnic pride, even as these are overruled by our spiritual understanding that love is irrespective of color.

This broom began to subside as family-first came into view. One of my daughters went through lymphoma, and it nearly took her life. I went on shutdown and had to get into high gear spiritually and physically to be there for her as she battled her cancer. Thank God that during that battle, it strengthened our relationship and helped us realize who was truly in our corner when things got tough. Before I could get back on track from that setback, my oldest brother took critically ill, and once again, I was in family-first mode. My books, my art, and even my programs took another backseat, just simmering on the backburner.

Broom Theory 4: Painting and Partnership Resumed

I had a bigger art warehouse and gift shop than ever before. It became clear that an art program was now needed, but also we felt the need to bring what we had as a couple to the community where we live, which is in great need to lift our children out of poverty and *miseducation* and to bring back the wisdom of the elders in our community.

As in Broom Theory II, my husband and I worked together to keep our family afloat, and we survived with trade and communication skills that are today so missing in our community.

Angelia's Black Love and a Cup of Coffee,
stainless cup by Imhotep

The Power of Words in My Early Life

School, home, and church was the order of the day for most of us Baby Boomers, and school was a way of life that I loved. It was a great replacement for the things that one may or may not have at home. Even being a part of a system that was segregated, it felt like it was our own world (as rough as it sometimes was). There was the wave of laughter, the movement of dance, and the feel of love—and of course, the occasional anger that could take your breath away *literally*, for I lived in the midst of *Fifth Ward, Texas.*

The first time I heard it called that was when I was attending a program at a high school for the last child to graduate from what was the "last page of segregated schools." A voice rang out over the speaker: "I am from Fifth Ward, Texas!" she said with pride. Yes, there was a pride that came out of Fifth Ward that spews out the great African Americans who are the first black to do one thing or another. It was also the side that led to the streets of nightlife and even death. Many took their last breath on the streets of Fifth Ward.

Lyons and Jensen were the two best-known streets, and of course each had a movie theater, which was the one place other than church that young black people frequented. Of course, we would occasionally see the nightlife people and great performers entering the Club Matinee: B.B. King, Bobby Blue Bland, and so on. Well, I never saw them, for I was not allowed on Lyons or Jensen after dark! But my brothers, who shined shoes and sold newspapers there, saw more than their share. This later helped influence them to the streets and the lifestyle of "the famous and the incarcerated." But thanks to the prayers and the belief in "teach a child in the way he should go and he will not depart" ... or at least he will return to the principles of his upbringing, and so they did. My beloved mother did her part in teaching and praying for us all.

The one lesson I got from that experience: it is best if at all possible to keep young people away from environments that would teach them an occupation that would lead to crime or a lifestyle that could bring unwanted elements into their lives. There was not much to offer in those days; in our neighborhood there were no front yards—the houses were so close to the street, if you had long legs and sat on the porch, you could nearly put your feet on the street. Still, I attended high school with some of the most physically gifted, musically talented, and the brightest minds.

You will find me referring many times to the *power of words;* it is one of my personal callings, and as I write this book I know why. Words have shaped my life—and yours, if you will stop and remember the passage that says "be still and know that I am God" ... one of my favorite passages. We speak *into existence* every day what truly shapes our lives and the lives of our children, for words are magic, and we all are rich with the ability to dream and to tell those dreams.

Yes, dreams do come true, but so do nightmares. I believe that if we think, talk, research, read, and look for positive information and solutions to issues in our lives, we will dream of those solutions. And if we meditate daily, it will give us the space and time we need to "hear the answers." Sometimes these come through external messengers: spiritual guides, teacher, parents, friends, and even strangers. Praying is great, but sometimes it can become a way to beg and plead for forgiveness, for wants and desires, when God already knows your desires and your needs. You just need to ask, then *do your duty,* as a master leader I know says daily. To sit and be still allows you the sacred space to hear God, and then answers will come.

Today I have a daughter who plays a great role in "paying it forward." She is a very special and caring person to the homeless, and especially to those who suffer the ills of mismanagement of their finances, be they little or large. She teaches how to get back on a good financial track. She helps people become homeowners and responsible for their lives. She has blessed us with two of the kindest, mildest, most intelligent grandchildren, who already are inspired to help and serve the needy.

One of my daughters has taught children from every angle—from the poorest to the wealthiest—and has the old spirit of the teachers I remember from my childhood, who dressed, acted, and carried themselves in a respectable manner. They were our second mothers and, for some, the only mother figure they may have had.

Thanks to those teachers who supported me and encouraged me—and there were a few who challenged me and even fewer who did not give me my fair share. But even that was by divine order, for I found they made me stronger in ways I would not have known. I needed strength to bypass the naysayers and negative energy that we all have to encounter at some point in life, and they taught me that.

This daughter has also taught us to truly appreciate the beauty of love in the animal world—and yes, they too have little spirits that get broken—for ever since she was a small child playing alone, our pet dogs were her friends. I always say if she had had human children, she would be a great mother, for my *grand-dogs* are awesome! I get cards and gifts from them on a regular basis, and thank-you cards and gifts for caring for them when she has to be away. I just received a call while writing this: "Mom, Zin-Jo is not doing well; his leg where he hurt it is turning red, and he did not get up this morning. I will take him to the vet in the morning." Her youngest and biggest dog, which she rescued as an outcast pup, has grown up to be a handsome and loving dog. The name was to empower him with a meek and loving spirit … and so he is.

I am blessed with grandsons from my son, who are so versatile and show so much promise—one is directing his life in the art world, one is a great writer and poet who has so much wisdom in his writing as in his poem, "Broken Spirits," and one is already starting a nonprofit while in college to help the homeless. Their father, our son, is talented and can do anything he sets out to do. He was my inspiration for going into the art world as a way to support my mission in the community. It has been said he comes from a royal lineage! This came from a wise stranger who introduced me to the books *They Came Before Columbus* by Ivan van Sertima and *Sex & Race* by J. A. Rogers.

I love letters notes and cards that show true feelings, and I have kept some for over forty-five years. There are notes from some of my teachers, who wished me well as I graduated from Wheatley. I treasure their words. Only recently did I go back and read their advice and predictions, and guess what, they were "right on the money." The rest was left up to me.

This is meant to let teachers know they have a blessed position to pave the way for their students in whom they can see potential.

Dear Akua,
You are a fine example of a finer womanhood,
Remain as fine as you are and you will have given the world a contribution it is greatly in need of.
Washington

I feel you have qualities which help you succeed in your life. Good luck!
W. Counselor

Knowing you as a sweet young lady, having had you as a student in my class, has made me know that I shall certainly miss you.
However I know that you are going into greater and more successful things.

May happiness in whatever forms you wish, it truly be yours
Love, B. Smith

I have watched your growth with great interest.
You have demonstrated the ability to reason logically, physically, and with a degree of insight, and as you strive to attain the rich awards of life, always remember that happiness is not a gift but an achievement.
Bryant … Economic

Having had you in my class
Has been a real enjoyable experience.
I feel you will fit very well into this creative world.
But one must first of all know thyself.
O. T.

Here is wishing the very best of everything
In life to a well-deserving and wonderful person,
M. W. … English

Perhaps the duties as an S-3 Sponsor were some confusing at times, and more so during the preparations for the 1st, 2nd and all the countless city inspections. However, your sense of cheerfulness and good humor never left you, even when your hamburger had mustard instead of mayonnaise. Keep your chin up, your good spirits, and the best of luck to you in all your future endeavors.
Israel G. … Asst. Commandant

You are interesting and so nice to know.
Keep alive your interest in reading.
I hope your life will be filled with success and happiness.
G. M.

I want to express my sincere feelings on wishing you the best out of life. I think that you have the ability to do great things in life.
Mrs. W. M. B.

I have had many Sponsors to represent the ROTC unit in an outstanding manner, but I have never had one that I found to be as cheerful as you.
The best that life has to offer,
Capitan Sanders.

This is from my greatest teacher of all, my beloved mother, to whom I owe all my respect and the ability to "roll with the punches." Much love for her perfection and imperfection. It all made me who I am and why I can share my passion and my pain. Knowing we are all one and that my life could be the lighted path to a greater future is why I am leaving a *MAP* … Making Attitude Payoff.

To My Baby Girl
Dearest Akua,

Words cannot be given to say how much you mean in many, many ways to me.

I am very glad of your graduation, my heart leaps for joy.

In one way and another way it hurts me to know you are coming to a place to leave me, but you can't stay always.

I hope you all the happiness in the future, and hope you continue to be as sweet in the future years as you have been in the years past.

Hope you continue to overcome and strive for the most important goal in your life.

I know you know what I mean.

From you mother with much love,

Mother

My school days were busy with school work and my religious responsibilities. I was serious in high school, always working on some goal or project—as my nephews would say, I had a cause and always asked "what is my itinerary for the day?"

Recently, a classmate from high school saw me at an event and smiled as she passed by my art display. She said, "You were nice in school, but you were always moving opposite of the rest of us; you were focused and had an agenda, even in the day."

I found these notes of blessings and reminders of hope for the future and decided to give these teachers a public thanks, as there have been times when I did not feel cheerful or on point, and notes of encouragement meant as much as the many wonderful letters Ms. D. sent me over the years.

This gives me the opportunity to say it would be a good idea to get people who like you and want the best for you to give you notes of encouragement. There will be days that these notes will make a difference.

I encourage teachers, pastors, and anyone who can write an encouraging note to a student, friend, or acquaintance, to do so. It could be the candle that lights their day.

There have been days I have felt defeated, mainly because I had let down my guard and did not know *The Four Agreements*, a book by Don Miguel, as I know them today, but I do believe they were a part of my psyche as I learned to get over negative words that cut like a knife.

When Words Cut Like a Knife

When words cut like a knife,
The blood of emotion is our life.
Don't tell me anything that you may regret,
Just look at me and know that God is not through with me yet.
Give me words of courage; they are food to my soul.
On days of darkness and white-out, they give light for me to hold.
So thanks to all the teachers and my sweet Mother Dear
For giving me these words that have lasted over forty-six years.

Sculpture iron Auk by Imhotep, Clifford candles

Be a Candle or a Match

I thought of what it's like to be a match.
The head so big and bold.
It is the match that once it's lit burns up it's soul.
It lights it's object and it's self ablaze.
It ends it's life in a rubble of black ash.
It has given it's all … in a quick flash!
A candle has more dignity, as it's served by a flame.
This means when it's lit, it has someone to blame.
The candle can do just like a match,
As it lights it's object, it gives a little bit of wax,
Touching each with it's identity,
Yet lighting the way for you and me.
It eventually dies out in a slow melting way.
But look how many lights and fires
It can give in one day.
Yes, I would rather be a candle, giving my light in dignity,
But without the wild, fast-burning match,
Where would the candle be?

CD Poetry by Akua

Akua's Gumbo of Life: Healing Broken Spirits (HBS)

As far back as I can remember, between the ages of four and five, I communicated with the "Universe." My universe was everything I could touch, feel, taste, hear, and communicate. (My all-time favorite thing was communicating—even as a small child, I was concerned about "issues.")

Standing in the middle of Taylors Court in Fifth Ward, Texas, I recall looking up at the clouds, as I did many days (I could imagine the shapes to be different animals or people). My thought process was beyond my years. I questioned who am I? Who were the people around me? Could we be connected? That question is being answered over sixty years later!

As the tenth child born into a family like many in Fifth Ward, I was in for a life of "Gumbo," a term I created for a nighttime talk show when the subject was whatever the callers wanted to talk about. Even though I do not like regular gumbo, the idea of such a mix brings many topics to choose from.

Power of Positive Words

My mother gave me my first positive affirmation about my health. The doctor who delivered me, told her I was the healthiest baby he had seen in a very long time. This important information laid the groundwork for self-confidence, to never fear helping the sick. I have stood on that positive message that was given me, and I am sure my mother did not know how it would mold my mindset about my health and carry me through life believing and affirming that I would not fear catching cold, flu, or even AIDS as it came out, with the fear of breathing near or touching anyone who may have the virus.

It makes me wonder how our present-day society would be if parents gave their children words of praise and positive affirmation to carry in their minds as they grew up.

What we called the Village also took a great part in shaping my life. In particular there was a couple, Mr. Otis and Mrs. Ollie Dees. (We all called the man and his wife by *her* first name.) They would allow me to clean and dust to make extra money. I was only about eight years old, but I discovered that furniture polish really gave their leather shoes a great shine!. Yes, well … But they never made me feel I had done something wrong; instead, they used the incident to tell me I was very creative and smart. I hung on to that piece of positive description; it has been another one of the things that I use to move forward in life. In many ways, I believe these kinds of people were *purposely* placed in my life as "SEEDS"—***s****pecial* ***e****ndearments* of ***e****vidence* can ***d****irect* one's ***s****pirituality.*

The question is: What SEEDS are you planting in the life of a child—or even an adult? It is never too late to be given encouragements or compliments that give us hope to do better. Please plant SEEDS, for your children, family, friends, and even strangers come into our lives for reasons. This SEED process is connected to a "universal law" that states what you *give out* is what you get back.

I was told by a woman, Marylyn W., that one positive thought makes a thousand positive vibrations. That gave me motive enough to keep on being positive. And she also added *the best way to* not *give enemies power over you is by* not *calling their names.*

I believe that is a good piece of advice, and at this age, I will take that SEED and water it in my spirit and use it—life is full of people that should sometimes remain nameless in our lives as we go through the valleys of life.

The Storyteller/plate by Akua

HBS and Negative Results of Allowing Our Minds to Be Vessels of Hate

It has been brought to my attention that dialoguing with people who may become friends is one of the ways to heal our spirits, especially if we are seeking healing and love and speaking in truth. This is what true, new friendship can bring.

We begin to heal as we dialogue in honest conversation. We cannot carry words of negative energy around with us on a daily basis, spewing out the verbal venom on a daily basis. We have the God-given right to be for peace and love, but when we translate it into the negative, we become ingrained with the venom that we carry around in our minds, and then we begin to attract that which we hate, like a magnet draws metal to its surface.

Words have energy, and words that carry the weight of hate, hurt, shame, pain, and distrust are heavy. If I drew a scale of words, the hateful words would outweigh the words of love, joy, kindness, and trust, because these words are very light.

> *With love there is no burden ... With hate there is much trauma to the spirit.*
>
> —AF

When our burden is light, we can move and excel faster to overcome our challenges.

In conversation with a new friend, who happens to be white, we shared our desire to get rid of prejudice and hate from our lives. I began to explain how important it is for us to look into the energy we draw by the words we use, how our efforts to show constant wrongdoing and evil deeds can have a reverse effect on our minds, as we become so ingrained to seeing and discussing the pains of hate. The more we talk about the "look how you have done me wrong," the more the shield of protection comes up, like how a turtle being attacked goes into his protective shield to become safe. In the same way, people see words of wrongdoing, hate, and prejudice as fiery darts coming to attack, and they also put up a shield of protection. Sometimes when I give this example, it is so powerful that people get it in such a way that it shocks them into JOCA—the journey of change and acceptance.

I think back to the days when I was feeling so much passion around all the new knowledge while first learning about my history and my culture. It was such good news to learn we were from a grand culture, that we had been so much more than enslaved victims. But it also made me feel waves of anger and sadness—not just for what had happened to my people, but that the history had been buried, that so few of us knew this! I had been an avid reader in school; it was the one thing, other than the will of God inside me, that gave me the desire to do better, learn better, and be better. Out of all the books I had read, *none* told me about my history.

It all started out with a cassette tape. I was thirty-nine years old, two of our three children were in college, and I had begun to feel something was missing in my life. It wasn't about my now twenty-year marriage; that was doing fine. It was that *my spirit was hurting*. That is how I explained the unhappiness that I could not express by any other words. I did not think that if my spirit was hurting, then it had to be damaged or in need of repair. I was faithfully married and going to church, so how could this be?

The cassette tape had been sent to my daughter by a young male friend of hers in Detroit, Michigan. The best thing I ever got from Detroit was that cassette! It was a speech by Ivan van Sertima. My daughter was not interested in it, so she gave it to me, and one day, I was cleaning the kitchen and decided to give the tape a try. Before it was over, I had stopped cleaning and was sitting at the table, dazed by the verbal blows of historical information, which hit me like an invisible bomb out of nowhere. Now I was a casualty of a war that I could not explain, because all my injuries were to my mind, my heart, and my soul. Where had I been all these years not to have known this?

I had not finished college, as I had chosen to marry and start a family and *then* search for my occupation of choice, in that order. And I had already started my design and remodeling business. My mind began to drift back to when I was a young girl.

I had been aware of my passion for design, art, and décor since I was a little girl changing my mother's furniture around every chance I got, using my lunch allowance to buy little cheap items from the five-and-ten-cent store (now called the Dollar Store!) to enhance my mother's house. I recall cleaning some of our neighbors' houses with my friends. I would help them clean house so I could change some of the things around—their mothers knew me and did not seem to mind!

My first job of this sort was when I was about eight or nine years old. There was this couple who had no children at home; they had an older son, but he lived with a relative (he may have been a stepson; I remember him as tall, dark, and handsome). I would clean their house and try different things—like polishing their shoes with furniture polish. I think of that now and how we as a nation have specialized everything, so that there is a special oil for our floors, our furniture, our doors and windows, and so forth. Well, they bragged about how smart I was to discover that Old English Furniture Polish did wonders for Mr. Otis's leather shoes and Mrs. Otis's high heels. It made me feel creative, and to be paid for the work gave me a sense of pride. Besides, I could use the money to help Mother—there was always a need for money and, many times, food.

Anyway, one thing that I knew was my newfound belief would be my new way of life. I trusted what van Sertima was saying; it made way more sense than what I had grown up being taught—not just in school about history but also in church; most of the sermons were 60 or 70 percent "Repent!" Or hollering and moaning. I didn't like that style. I liked classroom-style preaching. I wanted to learn and was serious even as young child. I really wanted to learn.

I remember a Baptist minister when I was a child. I can recall his style of preaching: he would hold his ear and yell over and over. I never could understand the intention of that kind of preaching, but it seemed to make the congregation happy and shout; some would pass out. But I wanted to communicate in a way I could understand the *logic* of what I was being told.

I guess my mother was looking for answers as to *why were we born*. She was ultimately turned off by the idea of answers to a much-needed question and left the Baptist church, looking for a better way to serve

God. My uncle and other ministers seemed not to have any help for a widow who was searching for truth and struggling alone with five children at home with no one to turn to. Except God. And so that is what she did.

Part of 5 ft. art Coffee/love/jazz by Akua

Be Definite in What You Ask For

My mind snapped back to the tape of van Sertima that I had just listened to. What was I to do?

I had already become unhappy with the church and its too-slow movement away from racism and prejudice. I recall crying and praying for a black minister … and then we were sent two. But in both cases, it was no better; in many ways, it was worse. For the first time in my life, I was threatened with being thrown out of the church. To be thrown out of the church is to be excommunicated. In the case of the ministry, if they were to be brought on the carpet, they would be placed lower in status (demoted) or moved to another town (relocated) to start over in a new "sister" church. What had I done? You might well ask.

When I was seventeen, we got our first black minister. His wife seemed older than he, but we later found out she was sick with cancer. I had no idea it was a *problem* for him, but I would have to get up during services and help my sister with her six children to the restroom, as her husband was not a member and she needed help with five boys and one girl. So I would go down the aisle during the service sometimes. He found it disturbing, so he went to my mother and complained that I was wearing my skirt too tight! I threw it away—a perfect gray-and-burgundy plaid, straight skirt with matching vest. I can see that outfit today as clear as if I still owned it.

When my mother told me after we got home what this minister had said, I stood up and placed my hands on the waistband of the skirt and turned the skirt around several times without it being stopped. "This is not a tight skirt," I said, with hurt and feelings of humiliation, and my mother agreed. We also agreed the problem was his. I got rid of the garment but never felt the same around him and chose not to be in his company.

The next black minister we had was sent to us from out of state. He had a great family, and they brought a certain *style* with them. They had just purchased all new furniture, which was being delivered directly from the furniture mill. I had never before met anyone who owned a white couch, and this one went around the room. It was beautiful! I was excited to see "one of us having something." It set a standard that seemed to inspire other members of the church's black membership to spruce up, and they began to decorate their homes. Our association with the ministry was rare until the black minister and his family moved to Houston. I felt that was a good thing, in many ways—to improve standards among black members.

The minister was very nice, and his wife was friendly and outgoing too, but as fate would have it, my spouse and I were not a part of the church's *social club*. We tended to stay close to home and were more apt to stay home and work around the house than to go out. As small gatherings and parties began to take place, no longer was the deaconess's home a place for the black members to hang out for social events. We were still not an integrated community, even though we continued to worship together with white brethren.

A new woman came into the church and befriended me. I will call her Nancy. I was a little cautious but did not listen to my first mind, which said, "Beware." But she loved to decorate ... so we had some things in common. I do not want to embarrass anyone; some of these persons are still alive, but I will say *things* were happening among couples that were against the teaching of the Church and the Bible.

After months of a growing friendship, it was not unusual for Nancy to come to my home and visit. She began to tell me of a friend of hers in the church that was doing some very unsavory things. After she explained to me the "big sins" that this woman and a number of others members were up to, I suggested she counsel with the minister. The only person I would repeat this to would be my mother; I knew my mother would give me good advice. I agreed with my mother that I could not do anything about secondhand information, because we believed it was up to the person who knew the situation firsthand to go and get advice. I did not know how much was true or not; therefore, it was Nancy's responsibility to handle it as she saw fit. My mother also told me to pray about the matter that Nancy would do the right thing. Mother further advised me again not to get involved—as I did not know what was true.

About a week or so later, I got a phone call from Nancy's "other friend,"Jenny who was trying to find out what I knew. I said I was not privileged to discuss something I knew nothing about. I was quite upset that she had involved me in her situation. I knew then I would have to counsel with the minister myself, because I was being brought in where I did not want to go.

Upon arriving to the minister's house, I explained to him what had been told to me, but he explained to me that Nancy had already counseled with him and had accused me of starting this rumor! I told him what had been told to me and that I had not spoken to anyone but my mother, and anyone who knew my mother knew she did not gossip and had only a few select women friends—and only two in particular that she talked to, and these were her best friend and the only black deaconess, who both had impeccable characters. These were the three "praying women" of the church.

I left feeling like the old saying *the early bird gets the worm!* Nancy's plan must have been to get to the minister first, and then she would have someone to blame for a rumor that was so vile that if it got spread too much, it would seem untrue. So I was left holding the bag, never knowing anything like this would be possible in the church I had grown to love. My husband and I would leave early from those house parties after that, when they became uncomfortable for us, which put us even more on the outside, as we would walk away in disgust.

I was, to say the least, devastated. I would have never thought this minister, who seemed to be such a good husband, father, and minister, could be led by members with that kind of character, but of course one of them was also a friend of his from long ago.

Lisa's Caravan to the Ancestors by Akua

The Biggest Trial of My Life

The biggest trial during my days in the church was not when my physical life was threatened by illness, but when my spiritual life was on the line. This happened in the World Wide Church of God in about 1980 … under the leadership of that second black minister. This is not about shaming him or his family, but I must tell my story to show some of the situations that can break and injure a spirit to a degree that never heals in this life.

A call came one evening as my spouse was home from work. I heard him say, "Please come over. We would like to talk to you too!"

The last time I had spoken to the minister was when I had gone to explain what was happening regarding the gossip about certain members participating in some kind of orgies and how I had been questioned by one of the alleged participants.

He arrived at our home, and there was an air of uneasiness about him. I had no idea what he was going to deliver in his message that night. It was a one-man interpretation of his understanding of my participation in the *church gossip*. But if ever there was a one-way conversation, this was it.

He began by saying we were a great couple and that he hated to come and tell us this, but had it not been for a relative who was a good friend of his wife, and others involved, that he would have been coming to excommunicate me ("putting me out of church").

I had not lied to or about anyone. I had not then nor now, thirty-three years later, ever had relations with any man or woman other than my spouse. I never stole from anyone, nor hurt or killed anyone. *But I was on trial to be put out of the church!*

He did not ask me one question, and *for the first time*, I really heard *and listened* to my spirit to not say a word. And it is so strange, but the times I have been the most quiet is when I have been the most innocent, and when I have learned the most lessons in my life. And this was a big one!

I had been a part of this church since the age of eleven. Four years later, we found out that a branch of it was located in our area, so I had been in this *physical* church since I was fifteen years old. I didn't date outside of the church until I was in the twelfth grade, and that was for a short period, about six months, and the boy was away five of those months in the service. I did not want to get involved with anyone who did not have the same values, so when he returned from the air force, we parted. And now, to be accused of gossip? Of wrongdoing? And I was to be put out of the church? Not the liars, the cheaters, but me!

Out of respect for his position in the church, I said nothing, but after he got up and walked out of our home, I closed the door, went to my room, and fell on my knees, crying to God. I felt so forsaken. Accused. I began to think about what my mother had taught me as a small child and on: how to use my moral compass; anything you desire to do, first ask yourself, *Can I do this knowing that God knows?* If the answer is yes, then never mind what others think or say, because God knows.

I felt God wrapping me in some form of substance, which I later found to be pure love. And it protected me; unfortunately, my spouse ended up being the real target of this plot to hurt us. He was angry, for he felt that he had allowed another man to desecrate our home by accusing his wife with no proof and no cause.

He was so angry, for four weeks he refused to attend church. Finally, the cloud of anger and hate was lifted off him as he saw me struggling to help him see *forgiving was for us*, not for them. I saw what hate, hurt, and anger can do; it made him look ten years older, a handsome young man wrapped in so much pain and anger. He finally let go of that destructive energy and regained his youthfulness and his ability to move forward. But he would never have the trust or comfort in the church leadership again.

I even spoke to the person who was a part of the group, who knew I had been lied about and falsely accused—I was a decoy for their games of sins. But God knew. And as in all trials and tests, there were lessons to learn and life skills to draw from.

I want to personally thank two of our best friends, for their love and support during this period, as they helped me help my husband get rid of the hate. He had to talk about it, and they gave us the gateway to purge. I also apologize for my purging on them so often, even though they seemed not to mind. Back then, they were the best thing for us, and we loved them as we sat and ate Ms. Mae's great snicker cake or even just buttered toast or an egg sandwich. No one could make buttered toast like Mrs. Mae—it must have been the love she put in it. They nurtured us and kept us from deep depression.

From the Mouths of Babes

One day, my youngest daughter, who was very observant though she was only four years old, was playing on the floor, and a thought popped into my head to ask her about something that had happened four or more months before the *biggest trial of the church* hit me. Our baby girl looked up with the biggest, prettiest eyes and said, "Ma'am?"

I had been thinking about something she had once done. "Do you remember the day we were over to Ms. Nancy's house, when we went into her kitchen, and you began to open up her drawers, and I was upset with you? You then said you were snooping 'like Ms. Nancy does' … Ms. Nancy was so embarrassed, she laughed nervously and said 'You know that is not true …' You remember that?"

I had begun to remember the rest of the events of that day. I was embarrassed at my baby going into someone's personal drawers and cabinets. I did not think to question her about her reason for doing it as I went into telling her how improper it was: "You know I have taught you to never open drawers or doors in anyone's house without their permission!" My little girl's big eyes had filled up with tears as if she had no idea that this was a taboo.

I had always taken pride in the fact I could be in a person's house for hours or days by myself and not open a drawer or a door without permission. Building that kind of character goes a long way, especially since I have been responsible for being in people's homes and had their trust that their privacy was safe. I never feared if a camera was hidden: with honesty, what is there to hide?

This lesson had come as a child, when I stole something once and my mother was so hurt. I never wanted to hurt my mother. And then once I took a small towel from someone who trusted me, again as a child. I felt the pain of being found out, and this cured me of that hurt. I had wanted to teach my children early in life about that respect and never to be a thief *on any level.* I shook my head, remembering the pain of having hurt my mother by my actions.

My daughter began to answer me, and she spoke very well, as all my children were good communicators early in life.

"You know that thing," she said, stretching her little hands far apart … "the one with the mirror on it?" She was referring to the dresser drawers in my bedroom. "Whenever you go outside to say good-bye to Mother Dear …" (that was what she called her grandmother, my mother), "Ms. Nancy would go into your bedroom and look into your drawers."

So *this* was the urgency of the friendship! Now I understood why the minister said she had come to him crying, saying I had gossiped about her … and that I was secretive about my business. She never heard me say anything harmful or derogatory about my husband (another little tidbit I learned from my mother—keep your personal issues and bedroom business out of trivial conversations with other women or men), and my relationship was never up for discussion. I was blessed with a wonderful relationship and felt that was a good way to keep it, by keeping other people out of my bedroom and out of my bank account. So she had gone looking for something …

I have moved on from that big trial and have used it as a launching pad. It used to be a stumbling block, but no more.

Now What?

When you know better … *you do better!*

My mind began to flow back to this new awakening of my culture, as I sat at the kitchen table, having flashbacks of my life. I began to cry softly, like a whimpering child, as my mind raced to the last thirty-four years of my life.

I had been studying the Bible and believing that the Second Coming was going to change the prejudices and racist hearts of those who, on a daily basis, were set to being superior and our "leaders." It started in the latter part of when I was ten years of age. *Now what?* I said as I thought back to the things I had wanted to do even as a young girl. I felt that I had a special talent and had given myself a name that I would be called one day. I would be famous (I could see myself decorating and my designs all over the world, for I would be the *best* designer)! I was designing clothes in high school, as I had learned how to sew without a pattern when I was twelve. My sister Ann, who used to sing in night clubs, would wear my creations. She had felt there was no way out after the death of our father, whom she worshipped and even followed around whenever she could sneak off. Ann was pretty, tall, and smart but was interested in the night life and good times. She loved her family, and she helped me through school, whenever she could, helping out with school supplies. She was very protective of me, letting no one curse around me or approach me in any way. By now, I was maturing fast, and her friends were always inquiring about me. Years later, I saw some of my very designs becoming famous. I was ahead of myself in my vision for fashion.

I also loved poetry and wrote it as a way to escape the sad times, times of lack, and then sometimes the loneliness of being the last child. My mother was sick so much of the time, and I had to learn to do many things for myself at an early age. It paid off in the end—it helped to make me self-sufficient while knowing that I had God on my side.

So … back to *now what?*

I began to wonder if all my life had been lived in a web of lies and hidden information in the church.

We were taught that we blacks were heathens. I recall telling my mother, at the age of about thirteen, that that from what I could understand from the Scriptures of the definition of what a heathen was … it did not fit the description of black people that I knew (at that point, we had been elevated from coloreds to Negroes, and a few years later, James Brown elevated us to *Black and Proud.*) Having had this flashback of my life as a devoted Christian/Jew, wife, and mother, and having even that go bad, now what should I do? The only thing I could think of was to check out everything I could get my hands on. What else did I not know? We were taught that we should prove all things, while also being told to only use the Bible as our point of reference. Now I could see that was like the proverbial fox watching the hen house.

We had somehow come to the conclusion that everything else was "of the world." I felt deprived and separated from my history and culture. I now wanted more. I had never really gone out and checked out bookstores, as we had an endless supply of books in our church library, which was a forerunner of the mega churches we have coming up so many places today, and they too have their own libraries.

I found out about a place in the community where I could get books by this man I had heard on the cassette, Ivan van Sertima. I was more hungry for that kind of literary foodstuff than any real meal I could name. I even began to do my own hair to save money for the books, which were sometimes expensive. I would smile and tell my family that I was putting my money on information to enhance my mind, my culture, and my dignity toward people, places, and things, by putting emphasis *in* my head not *on* my head.

I later decided to not use chemicals, which were definitely not good for me, as I could see what it was doing to my scalp over long periods of time. It finally came to me: "This can't be good for my skin or my health!" They are now linking these chemicals to tumors in black women—who have an enormous issues with tumors. I know; most of the women in my family have had to deal with them. As did I. After my second child was born, I felt an awful pain and was sent to a doctor while away from home in East Texas observing the Feast of Tabernacles. I had begun having sharp pains in the stomach area. I was examined by a doctor on campus, and a large mass was found in my lower body cavity. I was sent back home, which was the saddest ride I can remember, other than some of the funeral rides I had been on in my life. It sent my mind back to the birth of my second daughter.

We had planned all our children; it just seem this gifted seed had her own time in mind, and three months after my son was born, I was pregnant again. And it was a surprise, as I had asked the church to pray for me to get pregnant for the first one. I had friends laughing that I asked them to pray for me to get pregnant but forgot to ask them to stop! Upon the arrival of our second child—of course I had prayed for a girl, and a girl we got, a beautiful. slick-headed girl who took her time coming out.

I must remind readers that my church taught natural birth. Many of the women did use it, but some tried and could not or just did not feel it was safe, especially women whose husbands were "unconverted." One of my attributes *and* my flaws is that I will stick with something through the outcome. I guess that was the reason I never tried drugs or premarital sex—I would have been "hell on wheels." I always felt taking anything that would alter my mind was not something I wanted to do. Taking any kind of medication was something I shied away from too. So natural childbirth felt right to me.

Going back to this birth, it is probably one of the most important times in my life that directed my path to connecting with God. We were familiar with calling on the Elders of the church for anointing. That is what we did when we were sick or instead of or after operations. Some people felt they needed medical help but felt they were being weak or rebellious if they gave in to the "knife." It was easy for me, for I literally had made up my mind that I had no plans of being *cut*, unless there was no choice. But it would never be my first choice.

The first baby was so easy—I mean, miraculously easy. I felt I needed to use the restroom, but my sister nervously told me over the phone, "Don't sit on that toilet too long—you may be in labor. You don't want to have the baby in the toilet!"

Now this being my first baby, I did not have a clue. There was a doctor whom I had asked to deliver my baby naturally. He said he would, but that my husband could not be a part of the delivery. Now this was absurd to me—we created this bundle together, so why could we not receive it together? We conceived it together!

So I set out to look for a midwife. In the late sixties, they were not easy to find, but because some of the older women had used midwives, I asked around. A good personal friend of mine, Thelma, gave me the number of someone....

But back to the story.

Now, thinking back to the pain from that tumor, I had cried out to God to heal me. I truly believed God's love can make us whole. The next week, I went in to have it looked at. The doctor seemed perplexed. He said, "Someone must have made a mistake; you have no lump or growth." I smiled, knowing otherwise, as the out-of-town doctor had said it was the size of a football!

This was my second healing experience with God of myself. As a child, I remember storms coming; Mother would open the Bible and pray for the storm to turn away from us, as we had no transportation to leave town and no shelter nearby to go to, other than the church house. It was the only place made of brick that we could have been able to get into. The storms would turn away, giving me more faith in this invisible force in my life that I knew as God or Jesus.

Well … *now what?* was turning into … *what now*? What do I do with this information? What do I do to explain I can no longer sit and listen to untruths, or rub shoulders with people who feel superior and that I am there only to receive the crumbs from the master's table?

No, they had also said a woman's place in the church was subordinate to her husband—my husband and I cleared that up before we ever got married. It started out with the purchase of a tablet. Yes, a tablet. He bought me a fifty-cent tablet and himself a one-dollar tablet. My question was why the difference?

He said defensively, "I write bigger," which was not the truth—I wrote bigger than he did! I realized that the teaching of the older men in the church was that the woman was the weaker vessel, second in line and second-class, under the man to God. I knew then that our marriage would be in trouble, because *I* was equal—different, yes—in some responsibilities more, and some less than he, but I was not *less than him* as a human being. This was the first quarrel in our relationship. But because we were not in a sexual relationship yet, not until marriage, we were able to see each other in a clearer light, and not in the rosy but dim light of lust and excitement that makes things get out of focus. So he was willing to listen and understand what that fifty-cent difference meant—it was not about the money or the value of the tablet, for me, but the principle of putting me first, above or equal to him, but never last. And I was to give him the same respect, to give him my best and put him first. This way, we would have each other's backs. And it worked.

I stayed with the World Wide Church of God, the black minister had been sent to another state to pastor. The new pastor brought a new change, by now I was searching for more truth.

So what I did was begin to develop a library of black books and books of African culture, I wanted to introduce it to the church,so my first action was to go to our white minister, whom I thought was a great person. He was, but now I had him on a proverbial limb, and he had to climb down or jump.

He chose to climb down first and figure it out. I had so much information he could not deny, that he decided to take a course in black history at a local university. He learned quite a few things that eventually got him in a little trouble with the church leaders. There was a pecking order: evangelist, pastor, elders, and so forth. I got him to agree to having the first black history program at the church, which was over fifty years old and worldwide in scope ("worldwide" was part of the church name at that time), but it had never observed black history month. The head leader and founder of the church had died, and changes had already begun to take place. This was a mega *tithing* church, and it owned several college campuses and additional land. There was also a radio station and later television.

It was a mega-operation, at the time, yet because its members observed Sabbath, Jewish Holy days, and Jesus, it was called a *cult*, which it denied. I did not see it as a cult either, and I still don't, not in the negative sense, but it sure was on a new wave of gathering and herding the sheep.

Now ... the What: My First Story of Morale and Culture

The first black history program was mild and low key, nothing big and nothing new, or radical. It was safe.

The night before the big history event, many white brethren were a little uneasy, for this *was* new (to them), and many did not know what to expect. The night before, I had a dream, and it was vivid. I sat up in bed amazed at the detail. Until then, I had only written poetry, and it had flowed like a faucet anytime I needed to write it. This was different. I was asleep! But I recalled the story in detail, so I wrote it down. I even used a word that I was not familiar with, later finding it in the Bible—the word was *hamarabee*, which means *the strong taking care of and looking out for the weak.* I told that story the very next day, calling it "The Boy Who Had a Tail" The title was something I would play off of: did the boy have a *tail?* Or did the boy have a *tale* to *tell*?

English teachers love the play on the words that sound alike and are spelled differently and might mean three different things, all of which work with the meaning of the story. This was my first children's story, which I performed live, and it was videotaped during the black history program. This was a positive story that taught that self-esteem should not be our only goal; it should coexist with—a new word I coined—*God-esteem.*

The church was okay with that first black history program. It had a talent show with dancing, singing, and instrumental performances. It was entertaining. That was a start, but not enough for me … I wanted the *real* history to come out.

The following year, I had prepared. By then, I'd had another year of reading under my belt, plus I had started listening to talk radio (which I used to hate when my mother used to listen—now, there goes that word *hate,* and yes, radio stuck to me so much like a magnet that eventually I became a *cohost* of a nighttime talk show where I gained another family extension, a wonderful baby *brother*, Dr. OK, who is three years younger than me, and a beautiful *sister*, his wife, and a kind-mannered *nephew*, their son. who is the most well-mannered child I know, next to several of own grandchildren My "hating" radio as a child, due to my mother's fascination with it, put me right smack dab into the middle of it … there goes that law of attraction).

So … this black history required some real research for the information to be of value and our *true* history. No matter how devastating it might be, it had to be told. I had started a sort of underground book club at my home—not unlike Harriet Tubman's Underground Railroad, because the present-day enslavement is of the mind—to introduce some of my church members to the real history of this country and the African Connection. Instead of a gun, I used the *book* to help us escape the ignorance of our culture toward our true freedom of *spiritual* rights along with human rights. I began to go to programs at the Shrine of the Black Madonna; I joined a national group, and I began to go to programs throughout the area to *find myself* … as a black woman.

In church one Sabbath, one of the white ministers—just a minute, I need to explain something. Really, there were only few blacks who had the privilege to go to the church college, so the overall ministry was white. Not to mention, the requirements for black men were three times as difficult. We used to say, "A black man needs to qualify for evangelist just to be a local elder." I read *Sex and Race* by Joel Augustus Rogers (over three hundred pages in one sitting); I did not go to bed that night I was so hungry for answers to so many questions on race and history. My life was unfolding before me like nothing I had ever remembered.

Anyway, as the white minister began to preach that day, he began to talk about how "some people" were going to a *cultural shrine*, and that the church needed to be careful of the things they were reading …

My spouse was incensed. I was offended. Then the thought came to me: just as in the days of slavery, when two or more gathered without the masters, they would get into trouble.

As he went on into his sermon, my mind traveled over many situations that would lead up to this moment that I had been dreading—my leaving the church—but not without an attempt to leave some information for others who might want to do likewise. If the system was not going to change—oh, I could go on with many more situations, like how they called Martin Luther King a communist. Many of us, as blacks, were upset by all that, but we had held the church in high esteem, so we had not spoken out before.

We eventually had a black woman deaconess—one of the sweetest ladies you could meet. She had given her life over to the church; she served the black brethren. When the white brethren held a church dance, the first five or six years we could not attend. So we would move all the furniture out of her little house, even her beds, and place them in her little beauty shop out back. So there would be room for card-playing and dancing and much great food. I really miss those intimate parties, because they were well-attended, and people were on their best behavior for fun, good clean fun. She would attend the meetings about how big the church social would be, and she tried to duplicate ours in her clean and humble home. And she did a great job, from the antique crystal punchbowl to the silver platters, and once again, great food.

When we first started coming to this church, I was in junior high school and had not missed a day out of school. Then I would have to miss weeks for holy days, about sixteen or more as the Feast of the Tabernacle and the Days of Unleavened Bread were two full weeks of observance over in East Texas. That was the hardest part of being a "Christian Jew," as we called ourselves—missing school. Most of my teachers were sympathetic and would give me an Incomplete and let me make it up, as I was basically an A student. But there were two teachers who were horrible in that department; they kept me off the honor roll twice with a report card of four As and two Fs! Of course, I got grounded and was not believed, but I stood fast—as I do when I believe in something—to the death. (Later in life, that stand nearly took me out.) I carried myself back then in a such a way that the teachers would pick me to watch over the class. So I would teach the class and keep them entertained while the teacher was out. And I could hold their attention—even with all that I did not know—because I could paint pictures in their minds of the possibilities that could be.

So … this time, we spoke to the minister about the sermon and stated that we had the right to go and read books wherever we wanted to. Of course, he apologized, but he had gotten his point across to those who were afraid to make waves, particularly those who wanted to be ordained and did not want any blemishes on their record.

After that sermon, I noticed we were being *watched*. I had been doing Bible study for the youth, but now the minister's wife was always in the room, to watch me, as if I were going to teach some kind of heresy.

But I wanted to make sure that this black history program would *make* history. As it grew closer, I could feel some of the tension among some of the white brethren. I had several meetings, as I wanted it broken into three parts—one was "The Past," one "The Present," and one "The

Future." For the past portion, I wanted a black man to narrate; the present would be narrated by a white man, and I would conclude with the future.

When the lights were dimmed and the program began, there was a calm over the audience. That was a little unsettling. As they had entered into the auditorium, I had laid out two tables, eight feet long, with a large collection of my books on history from slavery to the high points of Egypt—now encompassing the whole Middle East. Some had stopped by the tables and begun to read, so they were a bit concerned as to how this was going to be done.

The first part was our past in Africa with all of its splendor: the pyramids, the beautiful creations, and the wisdom that came out of the African sensibility. Thus reminding us of our contribution to the world as a people, the Moors in particular. Then the white brethren brought us to slavery and to how we overcame through the civil rights movement. But this man made slavery seem like a God-ordained event, not explaining the many lives that were taken or the families destroyed here and across the Atlantic Ocean during the Middle Passage. It seemed as if we were begging to be brought out of an animal type of lifestyle and that we were better off and that many were pleased to stay slaves.

This was not what I had in mind. But I knew that this could happen; that was why I had arranged the event in three parts; I would have the last say. And it was just that, my last say. After this event, there was never one like it again. They did put together a few more, much smaller, but for the last fifteen years or more, I have heard they have not had any special black history programs at all. And I must say, the church has dwindled down to few people and into many directions. Not long after we left the church, it broke up into many segmented groups, as they quarreled over the great wealth of the college campuses and the millions of dollars in homes and buildings, which were left to be divided among those who took control.

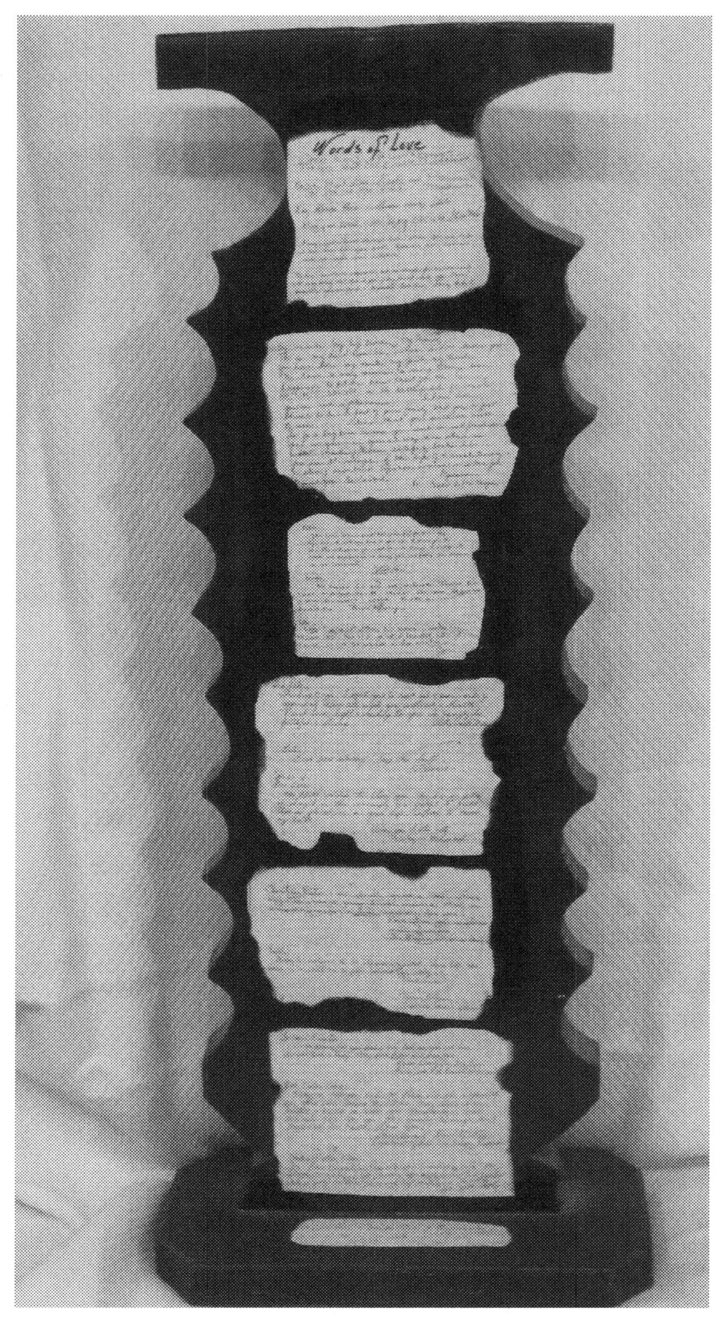

4ft. Kanara in honor of Esther King
by Jimbo Community notes of well wishes

Knowing When to Hold 'Em and When to Fold 'Em

This quote from the famous song holds true.

In the last part of the history program, I stood on the stage. If you can imagine it, the lights were turned down low and the music was soft and kind of fluttering in the background. The room was semi-dark, and many eyes were looking, wondering what could this be, the faces of people once happy to be just as they thought God wanted them to be: over every one, with the special blessing of Israel wrapped in white bodies. Then I explained the devastation of the use of just *two words* that caused so much harm and pain in some and the feeling of entitlement and privilege in others. Privilege they received either at birth or by the fact that they belonged to a belief that teaches *white superiority* as if it is an actual gift from God to just them alone … no one but them.

I do want to say, there were some brethren who really tried to be fair and loving, and many were as perplexed by some of the issues we were facing as the black brethren. I want to say thanks to one of the white brethren who understood what homeownership meant to keeping a family together, and he was a godsend to my family at a time when people who looked like us could not and would not help. His name was Jay, and he was a truly great friend. And there were others too, thankfully.

Sometimes as a healing takes place, the pain steps forward as a precursor to the experience, and if we can forebear the pain, we can reap the benefit of the lesson. I felt I was a bearer of bad news as I began to talk about the power of a name and the blessing that follows when we fall into the positive flow of words, having learned that speaking words is like casting a spell. It can be like magic, according to the energy put behind it. Like love. Or hate, which is really love turned upside down or fear.

After this second black history program, I officially left the church, to return only once in twenty years, when my brother who had been released from prison asked me to attend with him. I knew then, once I was there, that I had made the right decision and had not missed a thing, as most of the teachings had been dismantled and had returned to regular church teachings and observations of holidays. It was small and lacked the life I once saw in it, reduced now to a small gathering. I have not been back since. It was time to "*fold 'em,*" for I refused to stay and cause discord among brethren. The truth hurts, and when it is not time to be accepted, it can cause too much distraction and little good. So I moved on and bid farewell to all friends and family that I would leave behind.

One thing I will always remember: A friend said to me later, as she too had left the church, "I know your character, and you are not one to jump to just anything, so it was easy for me to leave after you." Had it not been for her parents, my test of being "put out of the church" would have been so much more difficult.

Leaving a church family and friends of so many years (thirty-two!) would not have been easy, but I had already begun to work in the community and serve where I could. It made my transition smoother. Some others who left later, and there were many, did not fare so well. Some became bitter; some gave up all that they had learned, even the good teachings like healthy eating and not smoking, and there were some acts of violence in some of the churches in other areas of the country.

I was glad that I was able to transfer my need for spiritual food into giving to the community—by doing what I could to make a difference. It is like the old saying: if you want to take the air out of a bottle, you put in milk or some substitute. That is the way it was for me: I placed community service in place of church service and belonging to a select group of people. Giving back kept me intact with my spirit of hope.

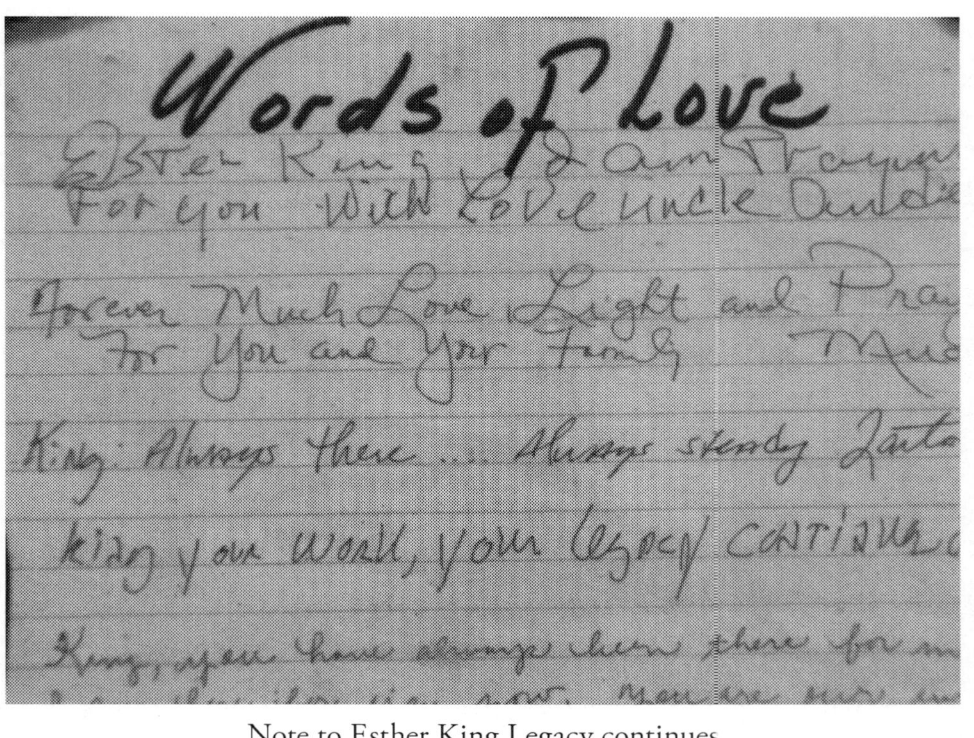

Words of Love

Ester King I am Pray[illegible]
For you With Love Uncle Buddie

Forever Much Love Light and Pra[illegible]
for You and Your family [illegible]

King: Always there... Always steady [illegible]

King your work, your legacy continue[illegible]

King, you have always been there for [illegible]

Note to Esther King Legacy continues

The Healing of a Broken Spirit

The next chapter is dedicated to Dog Lovers, and even though there are some of you who may not understand the love and the connection that some people have with their pets, maybe you will change your mind once you read about my Miracle. I got the little puppy that started out this journey of writing this book when she was only about six weeks. And I really did not want another dog after losing my last one. They have spirits too!

While sitting in a wonderful condo, fully furnished with more room than I can use, I have my miracle with me, my little dog. I named her Miracle. because I did not want to accept her after I lost my little Gin-Chica on my birthday two years ago, and because my relationship with the giver was not at its best. I did not want to offend my son, but I had no time or no desire for another dog. But I accepted this dog anyway, and she has won my heart. She is the smartest dog I have ever had, and I have had some smart dogs!

She started off by helping to heal my older dog, Gin-Chica's mother, whose eye care was costing me forty to eighty dollars a month, not to mention the pain of seeing her eyes closed and matted and her vision impaired. Miracle began to gently lap her eyes, one of which was nearly blind, and whiten and brighten their brown stains. Yes, she is a miracle and relates to me by sitting wherever I am writing and being a good dog. She is the only company I have had while I was writing this book, *The Healing of a Broken Spirit.*

This chapter is based on Akua's personal journey of how love heals, and it is dedicated to Miracle.

The First Visit That Answered My Life Question

The first visit was one of surprises. No one except my daughter knew I was going to see this Buddhist monk; no one there knew me. They did not have my name or any information about me. We had to sit on the ground or stand in line outside the storefront being used as a temple. There were twenty-four people ahead of me, including my daughter. The door closed after twenty people went in. We were given numbers so we could keep our place. We had been outside since four that morning, so we left and went to breakfast. We passed a Caucasian man sitting by himself eating breakfast, and he smiled as my daughter and I went by. When he left, the waitress came to our table and said, "The gentleman who just left has paid for your breakfast. He did not leave a name."

We, of course, were surprised.

The waitress began to speak again. "He comes in often and will select someone to pay for their meal."

The place had many people that morning, but he chose us! We were happy to give her a big tip. We had been blessed, so we passed it on.

Once we finished our breakfast, we returned just in time to sit in the row of chairs inside, to wait for the monk to come back out and give his talk to all who had been waiting to be seen on a one-to-one basis.

He comes out and smiles as he looks over the crowd, and he seems to be looking at us through a different eye, the one known as *his third eye.* He talks fast but deliberately, as if addressing specific questions some of those sitting might have. He is giving a mini-sermon to deliberately shorten their time for unnecessary questions. He goes on to explain how many of the young people here, who are mainly Latinos, are living a life that will lead to *situations.* He uses Whitney Houston and her life as an example of one filled with many blessings one could wish for—talent, beauty, fame, family, wealth, and even love from many—but she lacked love for herself.

As we waited for the delivery of the *personal* information, many in the group could hardly be contained. As I quietly waited, things would come to my mind that I was told by my daughter: that the monk would have different methods in how he approached his "clients"—some he would grab by the shoulders in a manner that an irritated parent would grab a mischievous child; some he would look at and beckon to come, as if to say, "I want you next," although that person may be fourth in line and holding space near the kitchen area, where the smell of mangos and fresh fruit was being washed. That person was me.

This would be my first time. I walked down the hall and entered a room to the left. I sat in this little 12 x 12–foot room, which had a tiny cabinet to the right wall near the door with cookies, crackers, and organic juice drinks all kind of piled on top of one another, not in any particular order.

To take my mind off what I would be told and how I would remember my questions or the answers, I began to take in what was around me. I sat and stared out the door, across the narrow hall, at a woman who went about the task of washing fruit and placing them in their respective boxes of like fruit; then a young boy and girl dried the fruit and placed them on plates, trying to arrange them in pyramid shapes as if it were a task of high performance. They would walk slowly away from each plate, and if the fruit remained, it was an accomplishment. Sometimes it worked, but sometimes they had to change sizes of the fruit to make it work.

It was kind of interesting, as it reminded me that sometimes that is the way life seems to be for us humans—as we structure our families, there are usually one or more persons that do not fit, like the fruit rolling off the plates—the oranges were especially difficult, as they were so round. I guess I was the odd fruit in my family in many ways, as I felt many times I did not fit. Until there was less "fruit" on the plate (family grew up and moved away), when my mother and I became very close, and then I felt that I had a good place in the family. Leaving those thoughts of family behind, I got back to preparing myself for my visit with the monk.

He walks quietly through the opening of the narrow doorway, blocking my view of the two Asian children stacking fruit. He smiles and gently places his hands around my arm and holds my hand after giving me a pirouette cookie, which I accept, despite *my personal opposition to eating out of anyone's hand, especially a stranger's.* But I felt this was some kind of test from the universe—those were the type of cookies I used to buy for my family on special days of unleavened bread, a special strawberry, cream cheese dessert that I had created over forty years before. You can rarely find them anymore all in one box. I wanted to pass this test. So I ate it.

As he sat me down in the little room off the long narrow hall of the storefront temple, he begins to tell me my mother and my brother are there. (He was referring to the brother who had died violently when I was eight. He had been shot in the heart by a marksman, and nobody knew who—my family had an idea but it was not proof.)

This was part of the question I had in my head but did not ask. I had heard once that we each have two angels with us at all times. I loved this brother more than my father when I was little. I guess because he showed me so much love—he sent me dresses through the mail when he was away in the armed forces. What I really loved about him was his smile and how he would show me he loved me in his manner of making me feel good. And of course I loved the goodies he would bring home when he came to visit. I do not recall my father giving me anything during those days when my brother was alive.

The monk began to tell me about my mother, that I looked just like her, about myself and my character. He said I was a very spiritual person, a good mother, and he said my soul mate loved me. He told me who I had been in another life, what country I had lived in.

Before I go any further, I must explain that my life for the last three years had been preparing for this meeting, People of Asian culture had been coming across my path; they were people of color who had been practicing Eastern beliefs or universal truths. (I write about some of these personal relationships in this book later on.) It is amazing how most belief systems and religions cross the same paths; the language may be different, but the meaning is the same. Such as *Do unto others as you would want them to do unto you* ... that is in nearly every belief system found. It is a *universal law.*

But this particular information about previous lives would only serve someone who believed in reincarnation. I believe I am a child of God of the most high and open to the universe, so I am not easily shocked at the activity of the spirit world ... or the many ways God can operate through his will. So if he can raise the dead, put spirits into wild pigs, why not *revisiting* spirits in new physical garments? I understand the vision of many—that we are *spirit* beings, having a human experience.

Second Visit and a Chance to Say "Thanks" and "the Truth Has Set Me Free"

Not having an address to go by but only the determination to find the portable temple in a small shopping center—in the wee hours of the morning just to get into the first group—my new friend and I and her husband were driving in two separate cars to make sure we found our way okay, as it was dark and early on a strange side of town.

We went back and forth, driving slowly, looking, and finally the concerned mate of my new friend said, "Is this it?" By then, we were already headed back toward the shopping center.

This second visit was so important for me, as I'd broken down and cried at the first one when the monk told me what I had wanted to know yet didn't want to hear. But it was also what set me free to finish the healing of my broken spirit, which had been disrupted as a child upon the tragic death of my father.

Yes, the truth *will* set you free, but sometimes it takes years to get there. In the process, you learn so much to bring you where you need to be on this journey of pain versus gain, the destruction of hate, and the construction of love. This, with the truth, is where it all begins ...

Sitting on the concrete with many of the locals and people from across town, waiting at the crack of dawn to visit with the Buddhist monk, this time I had brought my portable chair and a new friend, a young lady who had purchased my art at one of the Houston Fine Art

Exhibits. The painting was of an angel, a subject that you will read more about later.

The Buddhist monk would be teaching and giving away the secrets of the spirit world to those of us waiting for a "reading." No questions are asked, no information given about the clientele waiting to be informed. There are no appointments, there is no way he knows who is coming. You are given a card with your number in the order that you will be called to come in.

Getting up early to gather with strangers and wait for a man who has something to give you that can change your life around—if you are intuitive enough to receive the message—might sound like an odd thing. You may be wondering what a girl born and raised in Texas was doing waiting for the appearance of a Buddhist monk. I would have wondered myself only three or four years ago; then this energy of Asian influence and aura came into my life suddenly. I began to meet Buddhists everywhere I would go and be invited to sit among them. Some of them were black people, to my surprise.

One in particular was in her late forties and a deeply devoted *Hare Krishna. S*he brought her two friends from India, who chanted and blessed my art shop. I was a little uncomfortable at first, but I had long since given up on the idea that God only worked through one group; everyone has some truth, and much of each religion is more about culture, ideology, and being exclusive—and of course spiritual control (re*ligion* … to realign, set in motion).

Angel of Peace Health Love and Wealth
by Akua

My First Buddhist Friend ... for Life, Martha

Martha, a slender, average-height, attractive African American sister of quiet spirit was sent into my life to teach me some valuable lessons, not to convert me but to stabilize me and teach me the value of meditation, which I had never done. I had studied and prayed all my life, but sitting still for periods of time in the wee hours of the morning was new to me. It is beautiful to listen to nothing but the sound of nature and then the subtle voice from inside giving you what you need to know, answering questions that you have needed to be answered. And now, in the wee hours of the early morning, the answers were revealed. Martha came into my life to help me and everyone that she came in touch with. The last time we talked, she was concerned about me and my art being put out into the universe.

Martha's humble apartment of over twenty years was opened up to me as a place of refuge one time when I needed it to get away and solve some issues that I had to deal with. She was there, and her home held no art except her Buddhist pictures. At the end of our friendship, as she "crossed over," she accepted a little black angel from me. She also had a picture of Malcolm X, who was her hero, and a library of books written by a black man from Alabama known as the Black Lotus. This man was the first black man to climb to the highest position in the world of monks. He had passed the responsibility for his library on to her. Then she wanted to pass it onto me, but I did not like the books' covers.

They seemed to be like the white-hero superman type. But here was a true example of not judging a book by its cover. After her death, I did accept some of the books and broke down and cried, for they contained so much good information that I needed at the time. She left her writings about numerology in my care as well. She was the first black person who introduced herself as a Buddhist to me.

When she became ill and was dying of cancer, Martha's family and I were called to wait for her to die, as she felt the death angel coming. Her family, who were Christians, sat waiting for her to die and discussing her belongings, which they wanted to have, though these were not many as she lived quite simply. But she did have a car, a TV, book cases, a bamboo plant I had bought her, computers that contained my art, and writings that were for her "temple." We tried to get the information that was ours, but they took what they wanted, and as far as I know never returned my personal work or the work she was doing for her temple on the computers. She did take the time to download for me some important numerology that she had wanted me to have.

As they waited, they complained that the end was taking too long and that they wanted to leave to go home. I could not take any more of that kind of talk. She was so weak—the cancer had taken her down to skin and bones—as she sat with her elderly relative with whom she used to spend two days a week cleaning and cooking and taking care of her garden. Martha would make that trip every week, even as she began to become ill. No one wanted her books, her clothes, or her memories of family in the pictures she left behind.

A tin gift box I had given her, decorated with a radio sticker, with three fifty-dollar bills in it sat on her nightstand. Two fifty-dollar bills were left, but because they were under the flap, no one found them. Two other sisters and I had each given fifty dollars for Martha when I told them of her illness—graciously donated. So the kind and nurturing sisters offered the box back to me, and I gave the two fifty-dollar bills to the temple, as the members were the ones who had bathed her, fed her, and housed her to the end, not her family. The people of her faith took good care of her. Martha used words that have power; she took care of many people, and when she became ill, she said, "I will see if the rubber meets the road," and she saw that it did! She asked for assurance that she was appreciated, and she was very pleased with how they took care of her to the very end.

Her memorial was a great example of the way I want to have mine, to lay out my personal belongings and some of my art and have my friends and loved ones select a piece. As I looked at her meager belongings, I could feel the spirit of her and smell the aroma of the incense that she loved to burn.

The temple was full of her friends and coworkers, mostly her temple family. She was so respected and helped so many people, it was said if they could have had more people like her they would have soared as a temple, for she was their best in giving and serving. She served us all at the radio station too, bringing food to many of the programmers.

She was a gift from God, and she gave more than most. Almost a year after her death, I was moving from my shop and found a flyer she had created for me. She was always making business cards, and she even had begun a brochure for my art. She was the only person I trusted to write the meaning of my art, and she was so good at remembering what the pieces were—but she also knew the spiritual and the moral implications of my work, like no one else I had met. The flyer read, "Akua Fayette's Greatest Art Show of a Lifetime," and it was written in such a way that I could use it anytime. I broke down and cried, for I was truly touched in how she believed in my work and wanted the best for me. What a friend, helping me even after death.

My First Visit at Her Home—a True Friend in a Time of Need

I recall the first time I went to Martha's apartment. She brought me in the back way. As I followed her, she was dressed in a flowing dress, and in the moonlit night it gave off a soft, almost glowing light. The trail we walked on took turns like a long, twisted ribbon, and the path was green and leafy. She had planted incense along the path, so the scents were as beautiful as the still-blue night lined with soft clouds left over by the day. In reality, I found out the next day, we could have made it there in about fifty feet instead of about three times the distance. She had wanted me to have something to remember and to give me a sense of delight and peace through her preparations of insight and sharing of her wisdom and true friendship.

She took me in, almost a stranger, and let me talk and get rid of what was bothering me, as my soul mate was out of the country and I was concerned about his safety and our future.

She prepared her bed for me, as I decided to spend the night and she had to get up early and go to work. So after preparing me some refreshment and ice cream, she went to sleep on the living room floor mat. She did not have a sofa; she used the mats for yoga and meditation. That night, as I looked around the strange room with strange pictures of Krishna and images I could not define, I fell into the most comforting, soothing, and peaceful sleep that I had had in several nights.

Never Judge a Book by Its Cover

Martha's feeling that she would die the night she did finally happened in the wee hours of the morning, after everyone had left. And in her tradition, the body was cremated immediately. As I slept, she visited me in my dream—perhaps just as she was "passing over." She was in a red and orange dress, and she told me she would not need the things that her family "took" as she lay dying. She said for me not to worry. In the morning, I made a call to see what her condition was and was told she had passed and that she was already cremated. I asked what kind of dress she was she wearing? I was told a red-orange dress …

Yes, she did come to let me know everything was all right, and that she knew I was there waiting, even though she had been in too much pain to acknowledge me. She made sure to leave instructions to her temple members (sangha) that she wanted me to have her books and writings. As I said, these were books she'd wanted me to read when I first met her, but I was not interested in them because the covers with the white-looking hero-superman-like character turned me off. I had had too many white supermen heroes in my life, and enough was enough. I did not express my feelings about the covers to her, though, because the books were written by a great man—I believe, the first great black Hare Krishna—from Alabama. He had died at fifty and left a great legacy, and since he was her mentor, she had promised to carry on his message. He was the one called the Black Lotus.

Well, after taking the books—because she was the first person I had ever been close to that thought enough to leave me something—I browsed through these *Spiritual Warrior* books. What a surprise! There was so much I could relate to! Those books ended up helping me heal some old wounds that I had been carrying around for quite a few years. So yes, do not judge a book by its cover, but read the preface and browse some of the pages before you decide it's not for you.

Because of her beliefs, Martha's family was estranged and felt she was not going to be *saved*. They talked about her salvation, or lack of it, while she sat on the sofa with death hours away. Her family was broken, like so many of our families, because they did not live by the universal *law of allowing*—letting others live their lives without our judgment upon them, and loving them with unconditional love.

When I tell this story of my dying Buddhist friend, many people get the story wrong. Some automatically think that my friend is a Christian as I tell them how loving and serving she was to everyone she would come in contact with. She was at the top of being my best friends, if not the best friend I have ever had. And I had only known her for less than two years before her death. She did not ask to help, she helped—from creating business cards and flyers and a detailed brochure to working on a calendar, all for me. I tell them how she understood the spiritual and the moral intent of my symbolic art, and that she was probably the only person I felt comfortable to let do that without my input. She was always right on point whenever she wrote about the meaning of my work.

They usually say, "Wow, she was a good Christian," thinking her family was Buddhist not her. I would have to make the correction, and it made me remember my own judgment of the book by its cover.

Months before her death, she was still trying to drive out to the country and take care of a family member who was many years old, cleaning, cooking, and weeding her garden about two or three days a week. I remember offering to go and help her do it, as I saw she had begun to lose weight and looked a little frail, and I heard her mention feeling tired. Then she would smile as if to tell herself she was okay. But Martha? She wasn't okay. By the time she went to the doctor, they gave her only six months to live. She barely made her fiftieth birthday, like her mentor the Black Lotus, who died at the same age.

The Buddhist sisters of her church took very good care of her. They bathed her, fed her, cooked for her. She smiled at me one day and said, "This is where the rubber meets the road," and then she would look sad at the thought that there would be any need of proof that they would not care for her. But when your family forsakes you, the human side rises up in times of pain, with the longing to be with those who may not be there for you.

She helped me heal a part of my broken spirit as I went through a time when I learned a few things I did not like *about me*—I found myself with a temper. It was nearly the hardest test of my life, but it showed me how much we need to *become* the word that I coined in my children's book *Goose Sense,* that I needed much more *God-esteem,* because my self-esteem had bottomed out under the tests I was facing. But learning how to meditate, along with knowing how to pray, got me through with Martha's help as an instrument of God and her willingness to be used for that purpose.

To Conquer One's Mind Is to Conquer One's Ability to *Do or Not to Do*

I feel very close to God, I have always had that knowing of His presence, even as a small child and then as a teenager with raging hormones, which I controlled through the power of the mind and the concept that I had the ability to keep myself out of anyone else's sexual activities. I succeeded not because I was so different—sitting in the theater one afternoon and watching the big screen as the lead actor and leading lady began to kiss passionately (that was about as graphic as it got in those day), I felt this tingle inside of me in a personal place. I thought about it and then realized I may have an issue to deal with, and I did: I controlled my mind. (If only I had applied that ability to everything!) I learned to never let that feeling get out of control. That was when I learned that I had control over my body by controlling my mind, and that ability paid off later many times. I considered myself average but blessed, and sometimes I felt cursed with a mature body—which caused many disruptions to male drivers!

My niece reminded me of an incident recently when she, being three years younger, was walking with me. I was about fifteen, and a young man was riding his bike and staring at me when he rolled his bike up onto the trunk of a vehicle, which, thank goodness, was not moving. He fell into the street, feeling bruised and very embarrassed. Once we realized he was not hurt too bad, we laughed.

I had quite a few encounters that made me aware that I had to be cautious and steadfast in my position or I would end up like some of the young women in our community. To please the boys, they would give away what I felt was their most personal possession. I later added to that possession my mind and the ability to choose. So, no smoking or drugs for me either. I was determined to protect my *natural resources,* and my mind was truly the best resource that was going to get me out of the depressed lifestyle I saw around me. One has to remember, sex was beginning to emerge more publicly in the era for us Baby Boomers, but chastity was still being taught by those who were in charge of us in our community. Girls did not go to school pregnant back then; as a matter of fact, *the family way* was still being used instead of *pregnant!*

We also lived in a society that was still subject to the one who *employed* was the one with control. My first summer job, I was hired to help with the cleaning and organizing of merchandise at a giant resale shop. The manager's son was about nineteen, and I was fifteen. I was approached by this young man to go into the back room and have sex with him. I declined and left to go home.

After telling my mother about the encounter, she advised me to quit and not to tell my brothers, as they would probably try to do something to the young man and would end back up in prison. I recall thinking how just one decision can change a situation. I never regretted that advice my mother gave me, and I guess the ability to own a business was an even greater desire after that exposure to making a decision based on principle as opposed to needs. That is my first experience that I can recall where I had to base my morals on the need for money or the need to make the right decision.

But it was not the last. Many times I have given in to principles rather than money, and as time has gone by, it's become clear that whatever the money would have bought, it would have be gone, eaten, or destroyed, but my principles remain, and with them, I have been able to get my needs met with no baggage.

A Pause for Reckoning

My next transition on this planet earth is coming to its climax. What am I to do, for I have been on several journeys that have answered many of my questions:

Who am I?
What am I ?
Where am I?
Why am I here on this planet?

I am quite satisfied with the answers, and as I go toward my transition, the nuts and bolts of how I am to finish up my legacy here on earth are what stand before me. My questions now are different from the first half of my life and extremely different from the last ten years of my life.

Several thoughts popped into my head:

1. The first ten years in this time frame was my interaction with a Supreme Being on the level of questions and wonderment.
2. My second ten years was about acceptance of a concept of religion totally opposite to my first ten.
3. The third ten was building on those found concepts as they were being "fed" to me by someone else's mindset and reasoning, sprinkled with white-supremacist attitudes and agendas.
4. The fourth ten years was about learning how to use the gifts that God had given me and to use them for a greater good in the arts, writing, and communicating with others, while learning more about my weaknesses.

This point was when the s*** hit the fan in my life, now of activism, assertion, and the purpose of bringing me through the highs and the lows. What really was the purpose of knowing why I was born into a race so diverse and yet so tormented with racism and exclusion, though we had so much to offer despite the unleveled playing field?

Now questions and new answers began to flow like a floodgate left open in the worst rainstorm.

5. The fallout of the last ten years had played out like this:
    (a) to trust no man, yet through God's guidance, everything that I needed would appear,
    (b) the pain and the pleasure of the journey of life in this school of hard knocks, and
    (c) "where is the Love?"

This period gave me my third Dark Night of the Soul; the first I had in the second ten years of my life. The second time was death of my mother. But I had only just learned what "the Dark Night of the Soul" meant in my fifth ten-year period.

6. This is the beginning of my sixth ten-year period.

I am just two months into it at this writing, and I can already say it is another journey. But I am up for the challenge with a good amount of literature, friends, and energy to deal with what I have to do and what I am called to do.

Wooden Beads

I met a sister who knew more than me
about the life we live and how to be really free.
She had the smile of a saint, and she was nearly one,
for in a short while her journey was done.
She lifted all around as she rushed by.
She was in a hurry, now I know why.
Her family missed out
on the jewel they had.
They took all they thought
was her value, as she lay dying,
which was sad.
One of the many things I learned
from her living and her death
was that material things really aren't
our wealth.
In her living, she taught us how to give, how to serve all.
In her dying, she taught how to be brave and heed the call.
The wooden beads that she made, one by one, on a string,
the wooden beads she used to pray and chant; she did sing.
The wooden beads she gave with love.
The first she gave me as a friend like the symbol of a dove.
The second came to me, were made by her,
one of the few things her family left.
Given to me by a sister at the memorial of Martha's death,
who felt our friendship was far from mild.
We shared a higher spirit that made us smile.
The wooden beads are like life:
Some are bigger.
Some are smoother.
Some are sacred.
They are all round.
They are all wood,
with the same string.

Like us, we all matter.
Some of us are big, some of us are small.
Some of us have different hues and blemishes.
We all have the same blood running through us.
We are parcels of the same package.
Our depth and value depend on
where we fall,
where we stay,
how we act,
and what we say.
I hold the wooden beads each day.
Thanks to this dear friend, I've learned more ways to pray.
Everyone needs some wooden beads in their life.
Be you sister, brother, mother, father, husband, or wife.

—June 16, 2009

Finding the Black Angel

By Akua Fayette

My life as a child was filled
with the normal cares of
a child, not just any child ,
but a Black child!!
I saw no one
on TV
that looked liked me except
the servants and the poor souls,
who labored in the field.
I looked around where I lived and saw only
Black people. My used books were about the
lives of Dick and Jane ,
The only black in the book was on the dog called Spot , and he
was basically white ! I loved to draw as a child, but for some
reason* could not draw Black people, they always looked white or
ugly to me ...then one day I found me and my people...I found God in me.
I found the Black angel... I began to draw
my people with much love, so much that
their beauty began to shine
Thank God for Black Angels
I thank God for being Black
Thank God for You!

*Being of African heritage was not promoted in a positive light..it was used as a negative.
Black was also used as a negative , not knowing our true heritage the right

Rich Land *Revival*

Guess Who's Coming to Bible Study?

This chapter starts out at the attendance of the Women's Ethnic Dinner, the purpose designed to bring women of all ethnic backgrounds to get to know each other.

The food was prepared by the homeless and served by the men of the congregation, a very good event, but I don't know if it served the purpose of its intention. I was not able to see where it brought the *different* women of culture together any closer, since it seemed each group gravitated to their own culture, for the most part.

About three years later, I got an early-morning phone call from the woman who had invited me to the dinner. "Akua," she said with enthusiasm, "I just heard you on NPR!" She was referring to National Public Radio program heard all around the world. "You sounded great, and I loved your comment on the race issue about Obama."

For the first time in my life, I had taken the direct action of becoming involved in the top level of a political campaign. I don't personally care for the format of politics—too many lies and fake promises. I am a straightforward person, but that sometimes gets me into hot water. (But I really like hot showers, so I come out okay!) However, I really had a good feeling about this Senator Obama, even before he was validated by the votes from restricted white voters.

I didn't know that the interview had been aired so soon. She then went on to ask me to visit her Bible study group in Richland, Texas (we used to call it Rich Land). She said I could meet some great women who would be interested in my community projects to help make a difference in our community. I promised I would come.

Three weeks passed, and I had not heard from her, but one morning around seven, the thought came to me like a giant lightbulb had been switched on, reminding me that the day was Thursday and I should keep my promise to meet this group. I followed my "first mind" and left for the Bible study, not having an address but only a memory from over three years ago where I went before. I knew the street ran north and south, so I went up several streets in the area and found the church.

It is habitual for me to leave early for appointments, so I had time to find it without being late. Thank God I was not late, being I was the only "chocolate drop" in the room! Late is *not* who I am known to be, the trait of promptness something I practiced from a child, wanting to be a person known for being on time and keeping my word.

Now, over the years, I have learned much diplomacy in my communications, which prepared me for my participation with this upper-class women's Bible study group. I had not attended a "white church" in a long time but had much experience from the past, so sitting with these ladies did not faze me at all; it amused me, for I thought they were more fazed than ever—for what on earth could I be doing in *their* Bible Study?

As I had driven into the parking lot, among the nice expensive cars parked, I was waved by the attendants to leave my car—they would valet it for me. I'd never had that kind of service in any church I attended before. I walked in and was directed to the basement, where classes were held. It was nice, quiet, and about the norm.

An elderly woman was waiting in the basement; she was very friendly as she welcomed me to sit with her, but she said I was too young for her group. (That sounded good; I had not heard that in a long time, since I am usually in the older group!)

I remembered that I needed something in my car, so as I went back outside. As I walk toward the parking lot, I saw a striking, tall, older woman wearing a black hat, sunshades, and jeans. She was carrying an aura about her of friendliness and defiance.

She walked up to me on my way back in and said, "Hi, I am Shirley."

"Hi, I am Akua," I replied in a friendly voice as I watched her observing me—of course she knew I had to be … *new*.

She sat with the other lady who was sitting in the front entrance hall on a bench. As I went to retrieve my briefcase, which I had left earlier in the basement with the elderly woman, I came back up to the top level where Shirley and the other lady, who Shirley introduced to me as Sue, were still sitting.

I sat on the bench with Sue and Shirley outside the study room while the women's ministry had their prayer meeting—it always took place before the Bible study was to begin, they told me. The prayer session ended, and it was time for us to come in.

We began to enter the room. All the chairs were in a circle, including a couch. The women were very friendly and receiving of me. There was an introduction of me and another new woman to the group. I explained how I'd heard about the group and had been invited by a member of the church, who seemed to not have made it.

They thought I worked for NPR, because the person who invited me had heard me on NPR, and I corrected them by letting them know that I was a guest on that show, but a cohost on a local Houston radio talk show. I almost felt that I should have kept the radio show information to myself; I was not there to make anybody uncomfortable, and I'd seen the way Senator Obama was judged by association when he was running for president. Our show has had some of the most provocative guests on the subject of religion—some for it and some against it. As they began to ask me the time and the call letters of the radio show, my thoughts went back to my old neighborhood, Flower Village, where we had selected to raise our children.

This began reminding me of the time we moved into the 98.05 percent white neighborhood that was called *the Cotton Stocking of Rich Land*. The old but elegant community was filled with older, upper-middle-income Caucasians. Once we moved in, some came "to visit," knocking on our door, *almost* friendly. They let us know they already knew who we were and how many children we had. They left, and that was that, the only visit we ever had from that group.

Later during the recession starting in the early 80's, we worked through that entire neighborhood for thirteen years and built a reputation of the most honest contractors around. We had people's keys on us for years, in case they needed to send us into their homes or help them out while they were away. It is there where I really learned more about prejudice and "selective racism."

Well, I thought the white women at the Bible Study might be shocked at my radio show if they tuned in, but I was there for the long haul and curious about why I was ."sent" here. I don't believe in *coincidences.*

I had apparently missed the first meeting the Bible study of six sessions. They were reading books *on* the Bible and were just getting into the discussion of the first book. This book was about the power of the many names of God/gods. Just arriving, I had no previous knowledge of the book to prepare for the first lesson. I also did not know, until later, that the fee was twenty-five dollars to pay for a workbook and other materials. I was told later that it was free to me since I had been invited and the person was not present …

One of the first questions in the workbook was about slavery in the Bible. I sat mostly not speaking, since I did not have the homework for the first chapter. I was quite surprised how they went about explaining it. One woman was so impressed about the slave mentioned in the Bible who wanted to stay with the master. She was thrilled that she saw him as a person to be respected for wanting to serve his master and stay a slave.

The study session was … interesting.

They began to talk about Moses and how he did not want to be the leader, because he felt he could not do it.

My old church lessons began to pop into my mind; plus I had been writing children's stories on morals about what we call self-esteem. I could comment on this part as they spoke of Moses's lack of confidence to speak before the Pharaoh. I remembered that Moses had low self-esteem in his ability to talk and lead. But it was to reveal a lack of faith in God's ability to help us through whatever God expects us to do.

I spoke out on my concept of self-esteem. I mentioned the word that I had coined, saying that *God-esteem* was the ability to have Godly balance in our pride, which gives the ability to bring the best out in us when things seem to go wrong and to make us humble when things go right. This definition came out in the first story in my Goose Sense series, "The Boy Who Had a *Tail*."

They were very receptive to my comments, which were few, as I did not have the homework for that week's lesson. A light came on: *I think I know why I am here. I am here to learn something* (though still not sure what that might be), *and I must be here to share my experiences, being the only African American among them.*

At the end, there was a prayer; one of the women in the circle had confessed how she had not behaved in a Christian manner with her relative, due to her being frustrated about being diagnosed with *another* disease. Another woman comforted her as she pulled her across her lap, revealing the shades and the big hat being used to conceal her eye disease and the light affecting her ability to see.

This reminds me of my bowl exhibit that was still to come—you cannot judge a person by the outside. She appeared to be chic and graceful with the hat and the shades inside the building, but her aura was sensitive to her new news and condition; still she made the look work for her in spite of the diagnosis.

After leaving, I had my valet-parked car brought to me, and felt a little uncomfortable with this special service. When I arrived home, I was still having thoughts about this group and the fact that I had not participated in a Bible study for at least two years. I would have never seen myself in this kind of surrounding, having spent thirty-two years in a "white church."

My last experience of going to church was a black church. It was eye-opening to many truths from the Bible, but the overall helpless situation that was being derived from the studies were too much for me, to feel hopelessness in the belief that we could not do anything to make a difference in the horrible events that would come from the rejection of God's truth by the masses.

That evening when I got home, I decided if I was to return to the group, I would have to follow through and pull out the Bible, and of course face the previous lesson, which felt like there was something left out. So I had to go back.

I decided to go on with the second lesson and pulled out one of my Bibles, sort of brushed off "the dust." Yes, it had been a while. But first I had to review lesson 1. I did not like the situation of the slave position. I had been shocked that the very first question on lesson 1 was about slavery in the Bible. The very first question was "What Was the Responsibility of the Master to the Slave?

Mental Automatic Pilot

I recalled the many answers to that question and the focus was on the slave not the master: how admirable and honorable the slave was to want to stay after the master had given him the freedom to leave.

They talked of the pain and bravery of the process of piercing the ear as a symbol of ownership by the master—that is, if the slave wanted to stay and serve the master and become a part of the family. Each person who spoke answered from the perspective of the slave:

- how grateful and dutiful the slave was
- how brave about the pain in the piercing the ears for ownership

No one answered the question of *responsibility* of the master to the ones who wanted to be set free.

Maybe this is the real reason of my being here, crossed my mind as I thought back to the unpaid reparations that African Americans deserved for years of free labor, the inhuman treatment, and the many cruel deaths by lynching. This is the basis of why this country is weighed down by the sins of slavery, because the slavery in the Bible was one of *time limit* and one of *humanity*. After the time was served, each enslaved person had a right to leave, but not without being given generous amounts of the flock, threshing floor, and winepress … The responsibility was clearly written: *As God blessed you, you must give to him.*

I found it so uncanny that twenty women could read a question and not one realized that they had not answered the question. Yet this was a study, to learn and search the scripture. Sometimes when we are stuck in a rut of thinking, everything we do stays in that rut, and if we really haven't opened up our minds to travel a new road, we remain on "mental automatic pilot." I will call it MAP.

The Second Lesson: The Missing Question

The Answer Is Reparations: What Is Right in the Meaning of Responsibility?

I entered the room of about eight women, and as I sat, they began to start the prayer meeting. I was too early for the Bible study. As each woman prayed her individual prayer, a pause would occur. I was hoping they didn't think that I came in to interrupt their prayer service. After each prayed, one after the other, sometimes there was an awkward silence. I remained quiet.

When it was over, one of the ladies said to me that I was welcome to participate. As soon as prayer was over, about ten more women came in to start the study. There were two women who commented on last week's lesson. This was my time to speak on the question that had gone unanswered.

I raised my hand to speak. I wanted to use the most pleasant voice that I could, because of what I had to say: I did not want to come off angry, or hostile, and sometimes, because of my passion, that is something I am aware of doing. That is a family trait that I have work hard to diminish, and I so appreciate that quality in President Obama.

"Last week was my first time here, and I did not have the lesson that was being discussed, so when I returned home, I went over the lesson and noticed the first question had not been answered. The question was about the *responsibilities of the master to the slave* at the time when he or she was to be set free, or if they wanted to stay.

"Each person spoke on the strength and the loyalty of the slave who wanted to stay and how painful it was when the slave had to have holes placed in each ear to show ownership."

I went on to explain that the type of slavery that existed in the Bible was used to make people pay off debt, and there was a time limit of seven years. And one of the responsibilities of the master was to treat the slave humanely, like a member of the family. If the slave wanted to leave when his time was up, the responsibility of the master was to give generously to the slave, *as God had blessed him,* so that enslaved person, now free, could have a good start to provide for his or her needs.

Finally the silence was broken by one of the women, who began to talk about something else. She was followed by "Mary," a studious woman of the Bible who introduced others to the way she was a able to further her study with the use of a Bible program. (I recall some were a little annoyed with her efficiency.) She spoke out in agreement of my assessment of the question not being answered and went on to point out the importance of the master being a good master as God is good to us.

The rest of the lesson went rather fast. I don't know how my observation was taken, but being the only black woman in the room, I was aware that the biggest day of segregation is Sunday, and for this special study group, Thursday was also.

The change had begun.

I didn't stay for the service that followed the study group, but I planned to return.

The Third Lesson

I didn't make it in time for the prayer session. I had some "works" to do before coming, and I am always working on following through.

As I walked down the long, wide hall split by a down staircase and an up stairwell, I could see the stairwell was flanked by a table spread with four large urns and a stack of Styrofoam cups.

Sitting on the bench where I met one of the ladies the first time I came and who also sat there today was a woman who appeared to be of Indian background. Shirley called out a very friendly "Akua, come and sit with us!" as they made room for me to sit in the middle.

We talked about grandbabies for a few minutes and then it was time to go into the study room, which was like a large living room with a sofa, two club chairs, and a coffee table surrounded by straight chairs.

As the room began to fill up and everyone sat with their large name tags marked in bold print: Sue, Sally, Shirley, Lisa, Grace, and so on. And then me, *Akua* ... As music began to play, a calm took over the room, and once the music ended, the lesson began.

I made sure I didn't participate too eagerly as to "take up the oxygen," as a person I once knew who wanted total control of the meeting referred to my full participation.

In this lesson was a scripture that changed my life when I was twenty-two. It saved me from actually dying a slow and painful death. Eventually, I spoke up to share my life lesson of how I found out that *God doesn't half heal.* I shared the story of how after the birth of my second child, I could not walk or even be lifted. I lost weight and could not be touched; it took about four hours for members of the family to make my bed. Neither could I do anything for my new baby—or my first baby of one year of age. Upon reading the lesson's scripture, I had turned my face to the wall and cried to God to heal me or kill me, that whatever lesson I needed to learn I needed to learn on my feet, where I could care for my family. Once I finished the prayer, I could feel the bed being rocked as I fell to sleep. Upon waking, I could move my upper body, and in the days that followed, be led into a wheelchair, and then crutches, and then to walking in less than a month all, from that prayer.

"As Hezekiah prayed for his life to be spared, so did I, and it worked. I found God in me, and therefore God healed me."

The response was positive, and after the study, a woman came up to me and embraced me and said that she was so grateful that I was among their group … that I had brought so much to them.

As I looked around, I felt that if only that one white sister could be enlightened by my experiences, it was worth my continuing. We both would learn.

The woman that I first met as I walked up on my first day Shirley, who had been so friendly, was now avoiding me. Or maybe she didn't see me standing as she spoke to the person next to me. I hoped it was that. But I suspected that my pointing out the week before that the slave question had not been answered may have stepped on some toes. But the real purpose of Bible study should be to bring out the truth and to dissect our own reasoning and search out for the true lesson to be learned. Right?

This week in studying, the many names of God:

Jehovah
Rapha, the healer
Halvah, the part of God's name meaning *being, to be*

As in *human being*. When we just say we are *only human*, we are leaving the spirit of God out of our lives. So to be human is to be without God's guidance in us.

I chose not to stay over for the lecture, and as I passed down the long hall alone, I noticed a beautiful gift shop, so I went in. There were crosses of all descriptions and sizes, books, jewelry, and so forth. So I looked for angels. I did not find a black one. I spoke to the lady in the shop and told her that I was a local artist and was interested in showing them my black angel collection. She gave me a card, and I explained that when I was a child I never saw black angels, so I painted my own in all sizes and shapes and colors.

This time, I would follow through, all the way to production. A new day, a new time … and I'd be making a difference.

Finding the Black Angel

By Akua Fayette

My life as a child was filled with the normal cares of
being a child, not just any child, a black child.
I saw no one on TV that looked like me except the
servants and the poor souls in the fields.
I looked around where I lived and saw only Black people.
My used books at school were of the lives of Dick
and Jane the only black in the book was on the
dog called Spot and he was basically white.
I loved to draw, as a child but, for some reason
could not draw Black people…
They always looked white or ugly to me.
I found the Black Angels …I began to draw my people with
much love so much that their beauty began to shine.
Thank God for Black Angels,
Thank GOD for being Black…
Thank GOD for me.
Thank GOD for you.

…

The Fourth Lesson

Bible study today and a birthday celebration for "Carla," who was a wonderful example of living in the now and not letting what seemed to be a paralyzed condition—which did not let her speak clearly at all—hold her back. She has not missed a Bible study since I have been attending.

Today's lesson was difficult for me, because I saw the raw side of what some people used to justify going to war—defending the "good" that the war brings to another country, how God believes in a good army of warriors, that war is necessary.

I kept mainly quiet until the end, and then I shared my thoughts of war—that I felt the battles that Christ was talking about was for a *spiritual* war; and that if we would get our egos in check, many wars would not be necessary.

The Battle of Jericho was used as an example of God being in charge. I couldn't believe that some of the women were sitting there trying to make the Iraq War holy. I made myself clear that I was not comfortable with war for the most part, especially innocent children, women, and elderly people not participating but being killed. And that I did not like guns or violence.

Upon finishing, I could almost feel the heat from the nostrils of some of the southern ladies, and an awkward silence took over. As I looked over to my right, I saw an almost childish grin on the face of one of the ladies, who seemed to be excited about my presence, as if Bible study with some of these ladies had been a bit boring, and she had been waiting for some invisible bell to ring and set something off! I had probably not given her enough of a rise over lesson 2, as I had for the first lesson with my disagreement over the question not being addressed on the responsibility of the slave master. I expected I was sitting in a circle of strangers who were mostly, if not all, Republican white women and, by "money standards," rich compared to me and many of my peers.

I truly had not come to burst their bubble, but neither did I come in fear of their feelings about my beliefs. I began to feel the energy of protection about me, and I had to be, even in the midst of a "white sea" of conversation, who I am.

The one thing this scriptural lesson also taught, though it was not expressed at any length, was the word *Shalom*. Usually translated as *peace*, the Hebrew word means so much more. The concept includes wholeness, fulfillment, completion, satisfaction, welfare, and wellness. What a beautiful word. I liked this idea much more than these brutal wars.

I felt like I was being observed. I am sure my appearance was one of discontent, as the war conversation was like a hot coal of verbal misunderstanding on my ears. No more war discussion for me. So I chose not to go into the worship hall, where all the Bible classes met at the end of the lessons for further discussion. Instead, I went ahead of time to the home of a lady named Annie for Carla's birthday celebration. And then I sat in the driveway of the gated community listening to Eckhart Tolle talk about "the power of Now".

I sketched the outside of Annie's house on a blank book for Carla, so she could read the comments from the ladies.

Once inside, and when Carla was rolled into the house in her wheelchair, I greeted her, and we began to talk. I learned a valuable lesson in talking to someone who cannot speak well: you have to listen very intently, something we should do more often for each other in communication. I was surprised at how well I began to understand her.

Once in the dining room, I chose to sit by her, not realizing she could not even feed herself! So I helped hold her cup as she sipped, and forked her food, so she could eat, but because of her lack of control, her teeth attacked the fork. So another lady said: "You have to use your fingers and finger feed her." I wished there had been a special spoon.

Carla told me she had left her spoon at home. I was frankly not comfortable putting my hands in someone's food and then in her mouth. So the other lady began to finger-feed her. I continued to give her a drink, and a few times I used a napkin to lift her food to her mouth. I was touched by the care it took to make this sweet person, who seemed to be an example to many in the room, despite her disabilities, comfortable. Maybe she was one of the reasons I was having this experience in Richland, one of the richest neighborhoods in Houston.

The conversation got into religion, comparing the Jewish faith and the Christian faith during funerals. I was still pondering how to feed Carla so it would be comfortable for the both of us. The lady to my left, one of the ladies in my Bible class, turned to me and said, "I could tell by your body language that you weren't comfortable with the Bible study about war today."

I smiled in agreement, because throughout my life I have been for peace and trying to use the *being* in me, which is guided by a higher power, to help curb violence.

Another woman began to speak, clearly upset, about how Oprah was *dangerous* because she "has a church" and that she teaches "against the old rugged cross," and therefore she is dangerous to masses of people because of her power.

Another chirped in, "You know how money changes people? Oprah has too much money!"

I smiled then, for I had never heard a white person say you could have too much money. Of course I knew, like many other rules, when African Americans jump in, the rules change.

Another one, across from me, seemed to be uncomfortable, which made me wonder if maybe my presence had suddenly been remembered—as I was the only African American, the chocolate elephant at the table. Or would the conversation have been far worse had I not been there? She took the conversation into a more positive direction. "You can't believe everything you see on the Internet. People are out to get Obama and anyone who supports him, so maybe *that* needs to be looked at, for Oprah has done so much for so many people."

I too began to think of how much she has done—especially for *white* people! They could never *truly* claim that she was prejudiced against them, yet they were speaking negatively about her, not taking into account the many white people she had helped make famous. Including the many white authors, many from whom I had gained some of the spiritual knowledge that had been hidden in ancient books of wisdom. I truly believe Oprah's standing up for Senator Obama was the last straw for many of these women.

The room began to feel like someone had lifted a cloud and the drop of chocolate had not melted or disappeared but was still among the normally all-vanilla party … then *oomph.* I could feel the energy level rise and then fall at the realization that such a private, gossipy subject had been exposed to the chocolate elephant in the room.

Someone became aware of my presence. She then added her own "Oprah has done good for many people" comment as a flash of redness crossed the faces of some of the women who had forgotten that I was at the table, feeding the birthday lady.

I gave my gift to the *young* lady for her birthday and had everyone leave her a message of goodwill in the book, to take home and create good memories of her birthday.

I left ahead of many of the women and, on the way home, had much to think about. I decided that I *would* go to the last event. Instead of the church, it was to be at the home of one of the ladies who was responsible for this Women's Bible Study program.

I ask the Creator in my prayers to give me health, peace, love, and wealth. I understood that the road to that prayer was searching my soul for *pain bodies* of racist relationships in the past. After more than fifteen years of attending services with only African Americans, this was a challenge to be meeting in an atmosphere of unknown expectations. I had no idea what they thought of me; they did not know me, and I was not with anyone who could validate my presence. Some may wonder about my motives, as a black woman, to be there; some may have been intimidated by my presence. But as the lessons went on, I believe that most could feel my intent was not to cause any trouble. By the time of the birthday party, they had practically forgotten I was among them, as they discussed Oprah's "financial empire" and her trying to tell people how to live.

They could not have chosen a better person to pick on in my presence, because I felt green envy here in this house full of rich women discussing a phenomenally successful black woman who had come from nowhere and had nothing compared to many of their rich pedigrees and family backgrounds. The irony of this taking place was that I, who came from what most people would think of that same kind of nothing background and poverty, had chosen to move into and then move out of a white neighborhood named "Flower Village", but known as the Cotton Stocking of Rich Land (countryside, upper-middle, and rich backgrounds).

The houses were mostly on lots that were nearly an acre in size. This is where we raised our children, and it taught them many things by just being in that neighborhood of doctors, corporate managers, schoolteachers, and so forth. I, on the other hand, possessed a different kind of richness. I was aware of my culture, my true lineage (I am a child of God), and the love and respect of a people who had far more value than even they knew themselves. These women did not make me feel inferior, for I am not, and I believe they could feel the aura of my essence.

But this experience was not over by a long shot. The last day, a big party day of celebration was coming, and I was going to follow this all the way, even if Jayne—the person who originally invited me—was never to appear! I often wondered if these other women felt that was odd too or even if it was a lie that I'd been invited. But by now I did not care what they thought. I was going to follow through … or was I?

That evening when I went home, I began to think about that day and all the days before. A month had passed by, and I had not seen Jayne. What kind of invitation was this? But it was almost over, and it was like a movie, only I was in it not as the fly on the wall, but the *chocolate elephant in the room*.

I had no idea where this address in Richland would lead me, but I knew it would be nice. I had become very comfortable in nice surrounding, as I was in the interior-home-and-light–remodeling business, and so beautiful, rich homes were normal. But a house full of women who were not only rich but connected by a neighborhood that had a reputation of wealth and Republican values were surely the opposite of my mindset and that of my peers.

As usual, I arrived early. The house had an open plan and was very nice—nothing outlandish, but good, nice quality, and it had a feel of a home, not a magazine picture of perfectly picked pieces. It had character, and the hostess was very nice too. I had no idea that so many women would be coming to this house. Women from all the other Bible classes began to file in; some were friendly, some were cool. It was fine with me. I had already determined today would be the day I would speak out to an audience that would not probably happen again in my lifetime, and today would be the day to "speak to the moment." There was food to partake as each woman scrambled to find a seat, which were disappearing as so many women began to pile in. I believe there were about seventy or eighty and, yes, I was still the chocolate elephant in the room!

The meeting began, and women began to speak of their experiences. One talked of a life-threatening illness that she was healed of, and she expressed the sadness, the pain, and then the joy of healing.

One shared her present health conditions and how being recently unemployed, she was blessed with a special job with clients who could afford such luxury of having a private shopper—she couldn't and was grateful for the job.

Another was heartbroken about a relative who was in jail, and she felt helpless. My mind began to question if I had really came into the richest neighborhood in town! But of course I had the right address … I listened to many more tell their stories and how grateful they were for being a part of this religious connection.

I decided not to speak until the very end. I wanted every woman to remember what I needed to say. If I had wanted to *play* upon this experience, I would have had a tape recorder. I could have turned this into that kind of a situation, but what I was doing was for real, and I was not there to spy or collect information and have chosen not to name the women or the church. But as I was told by the monk, I have a story inside of me that has to be told, and this was part of my unusual journey.

So at the end of this last meeting, I crawled over many who were literally piled around on the floor, in chairs, on sofas, and I climbed to the front of the room. I stood and introduced myself and said I had been invited by a lady whom I had met as an interior designer, and we had hit it off at a meeting I'd attended two years before. I had run into her at a local business in Midtown, and she invited me again for about the third time. So I woke up and decided to come one day, and then I could not stop coming. First, because I wanted to prove I was not scared;

second, because I know who I am and that everything that I do is not by accident—even when it seems like a defiant reason, it is always to aid me on my journey. I explained about my experience in Flower Village and the church I had been going to for the last forty years of my life, aiding, working for, and helping white people, and that now I was all about helping and aiding *my* people, who are in need of help in so many of the neighborhoods, for the *next* forty years!

Before they could make an assessment of that statement and what it meant, I went on to explain how, in being among them, I could feel their pain, their joy, their anger, the normal emotions that I see, feel, and experience in poor, middle, and now rich neighborhoods. I explained they were no better than me or me them, but … the difference was money and how it is used to keep communities apart. But all the money in the world cannot keep away what happens to all human beings—we are connected—and if we would put our minds, our love, and our money to work together, it would be a better world.

Many clapped and only a few were not so acceptable of my assessment, but it was over, and I was done. I was hugged by some and asked to visit—although no one has ever reached out to me, and I am fine with that. I love who I am and who I am connected to most of all, the Higher Power who hears the poor and the rich, and we are all His Children. We just need to understand the universal laws:

What I do *to you, for you, and against you,*
will be part of the return on my "interest" of life.(AF)

The end of this journey is one of circumstance, irony, and it is plain out funny! About three weeks later, I ran into "Jayne." I told her I did go to the Bible study. She looked surprised and said, "Good. What day did you go?"

I answered, "Every day except the very first. I finished all five lessons!"

She then looked puzzled, and she said, "I was there most of the lessons. So how could we have missed each other?" Then a smile and a more puzzled look came across her face. "Which church did you go to?"

I explained where the church was located.

A look of execrated horror came across her face. "That's the church where the rich white women attend! I would not dare go into that study!"

Now the funny part is Jayne is white and not poor, but she was intimidated or at least uncomfortable by the thought of worshiping with those ladies. She then said, "I guess that was where you were supposed to go … Wow, what a story!".

Of course I was floored, and then we both laughed so hard.

I had crashed the richest church women's Bible study in town! But I was so authentic in my personal belief of following through that I was accepted by many, at least to the point they allowed me to attend all the events and never had me thrown out or were rude in asking me to prove my valid invitation. To this, I want to thank them for "accepting my truth." Though it was the wrong location, I did not know it. It actually *was* meant to be, and that is how *divine intervention* comes, in many ways and many forms. *This* was my lesson, and I am grateful for the opportunity that was given and also for having met Carla and knowing her joy and kindness in living her life in its raw beauty of allowing and accepting.

I also hope I brought a sense of strength and truth in the stand toward the *responsibility of this great country*, which has gained that greatness off the backs of many immigrants and illegal workers, but most of all by the sweat, tears, blood, and lives of Africans brought here to slavery and inhumane treatment so some white people and the country as a whole could acquire mass wealth, and the blocking of my people from reading and receiving what was fair and just. Who knows how many Oprahs we would have if …

Yes, there is a *responsibility*. And there is a universal law that will see that it is done. It *is* done. It is already done.

A Nod to Oprah

I personally think Oprah Winfrey is phenomenal, as a single, black woman, no matter how some disagree with how she chooses to spend and give away her money. In particular, I am proud of her placing a school in Africa. I know many who feel she should have done it here, but most cultures send money and help their homeland. The young ladies who were chosen to attend Oprah's school were so deserving; many risked their lives to go, walking in the wee dark hours of the morning. Any child who really has the desire to go to school in this country has far more opportunities than the young girls for whom she made going to a good school possible. I really believe if you teach young women, you do more to create a greater home, which creates greater communities, which develop greater towns, which lead to greater countries …

Oprah gives away more than any person I know, and I say this because there is something she gives that is priceless. She has given the opportunity to the common person, if she or he will listen, to begin to reach out of the "box of life" by reading (and reading some more) and searching for the meaning of living *our best life*, seeing life as it is from a *spiritual* point of view, based not on religious dogmas but on the laws of the universe put into place by a great Universal Power, that some of us call God.

I started out at forty-seven, leaving behind the need for church to be my force, but trusting in God, who, as my mother told me, is always with me. Everything that I learned before was good for me; I still obey as if I were attending, because what is good and true … is still good and true.

For a woman who came to this planet via the curiosity of a young boy about what was under a young girl's skirt—that's how Oprah describes coming into being in her mother's womb—for a plain black girl, not a fashion model, from a broken home, moved about as a child and feeling unwanted, for a young woman who was given a second chance after the loss of an unborn baby while she was just a child herself, the one thing she had going for herself was she was a great reader and found being smart gave you an edge in life. She also was in the flow of her "hypnotic rhythm." As she began to use her money and power to help others. How can anyone not give her credit for being a Miracle in Motion? I am taking out the time to say this in this chapter, because I understand some of the envy of white America for her ability to beat a system that should have held her back—that intended to, down to its law of not allowing blacks to read. Oprah is a perfect example of how reading can give one hope and the understanding of how to not only survive but to excel.

I would literally cry sometimes at what Oprah had accomplished. I saw the parallel of our lives, mine on the smaller, community level, and hers on the bigger, universal level. I wanted to do so many things, I was full of books, art, design ideas, solutions, and I felt what I had inside and wanted to get out. And I began to get these things out in many ways—through PBS, newspapers, and other media over the last fifteen years. I am happy for Oprah and want to continue my journey, and I know the doors will open soon to let all this creativity inside of me out!

Once I left the church, I was hungry for more knowledge, and I began to read even more, joined organizations, went to Austin to see what the political world was about. I started a civic club (I had never even *attended* a civic club). I became a delegate for the president (at one time I had never even voted because of the church). Writing children's stories, plays, TV appearances, and newspaper articles on my art of symbolism—what I many times thought if *I only I'd done this when I was younger*—I found out it was not for me to do while I was young. I am here to give hope to women of older ages to never give up your desires.

As I was writing this book, I got two calls; each one was for a long-time desire of mine. The good dentist of our community was about to print a newspaper, and he invited me to write for the paper. The second call was the opportunity to be a host of my own radio show, and I would love to have a show that deals with relationships. God has provided these opportunities for me. This is what is known as *going in the flow.* I call it Following Love's Ongoing Wisdom, FLOW.

I am learning that even when we are on the right path, things will go "wrong," but that is just a warning that we have made a wrong turn, hit a temporary bump, stopped instead of moving forward. Yet when we are in the flow, the laws of the universe will be on point, whether we are or not, so interference can be and usually is a good thing. It is left up to us to see the light and know *things work our good for those who love God.*

The Dinner of Life

By Akua Fayette

An evening out for a meal of Hope
The menu was long and **grand**
The food was not what one would expect
It could not be eaten with **hands**
This meal was one of character as the rest was to **remain**
As the selections were many and were not easy to **obtain**
Beauty was in the foreground but was not the first thing on **the list**
Balance was delicious and wisdom was wrapped in **a twist**
With Courage was for the taking but giving it back was not **OK**
Harmony smelled wonderful as prosperity was on the **way**
Happiness was given in great amounts as an extra side **dish**
Inspiration was dressed fit for a king, as if it were a **fish**
Well-being was an extra portion that was stacked up on the **plate**
Radiant Health was playing softly as music while we **ate.**
The dessert was piled high with love and joy topped by a happy note
Finished off with a toast for a life of happiness started out by **hope**…
The restaurant was named Abundance as all who came were **fulfilled**
They Looked out the "windows of confidence" enjoying the peace on the **hill.**

The Breaking and Healing Events That Stand Out in My Life: Pain, Death, Illness, Physical Loss, and Emotional Abuse

Healing my Broken Spirit … for me has been many things at different times.

—Akua Fayette

The Darkest Night of the Soul

There is nothing like what is called "the darkest night" of the soul. It is when you go through a pain so great, the strongest feelings of hate, anger, revenge, depression, anxiety, bewilderment, disgust, betrayal, or sheer fear come into your life. Sometimes these emotions come in multiple waves, and sometimes they take turns visiting you during the time of the trials, hardships, rejections, and abandonment.

1. Mine started at birth, and I was just the *recipient* of an issue that was to be my platform to start my life's journey on its way to get my soul to "recover" and to find my truth.
2. Ages 05 years taught me that neighbors are important and can have a positive or negative effect on your life. I grasped the lesson they brought me at a very young age, and the lessons stayed with me.

3. At the tender age of five, my journey took a great leap into the world of "renter's demise," with the events of having to move from pillar to post.

The many hard and sometimes devastating moves amounted to about every two to three months for five years, until the final move when my father left us homeless and landed my mother and four of us children at my mother's sister's. Our aunt's house was a two-bedroom duplex, shotgun, but extremely neat and well-decorated. She was an awesome person in many ways, and what she could do with a needle and thread, crochet, hammer and nails, and garden tools was phenomenal. This had to be a challenge for her tender nerves.

4. The pain of leaving my friends, young and old, was the biggest lesson that shaped my mind toward homeownership for my family and to never have to depend on someone else for shelter. In our case, it led to an early death for my father. This death made greater breakage in an already broken family in ways we are still having to deal with—the downside of living through that tragic loss.

5. The next one (this actually happened two years before my father's death) was the death of my beloved oldest brother, who started out being angry about my mother's pregnancy with me and grew to be the sibling who gave me the most love as a child. He never forgot me, sending me dresses from the air force, and he was my hero. He was taken away from us by a sniper's bullet.

6. Not every death in a family leaves you broken, but sometimes just sad and hurt, or a feeling of loneliness. And of course, there were quite a few of those along the way. But the one that resolved an old pain, even as it brought new pains, was my father's tragic death at the hands of my beloved aunt, my mother's sister. I was there, and the only good thing that came out of that experience was that my daddy was inspired to pick me up and take me into his arms and say, "Daddy loves you"! In what seemed like less than a minute, he was gone with the firing of the gun in one shot.

Those last words he spoke to me stayed with me for years and would comfort me when the painful "sorry baby, Daddy forgot about you" feelings would come to sadden me during my journey. He did love me. I needed to know that. I would later find out why.

About three years after my father's death, the aunt who took his life, out of fear and a nervous condition, was getting her life back in order, and she and my mother, who were once the best example I have seen of sisters, were able to be together and mend the pain they both felt over such a tragic death, which had broken them apart for a short while. As they regained their relationship, my aunt moved once again, though not too far, as they always liked living near each other. Within months of her new move, she had a terrible accident. She had a seizure and fell into water that had been running for her bath. Due to the water heater being outside in the sun, the water temperature was extremely hot, and she passed out in the water and received third degree burns over most of her body. Five days later, she died in the hospital.

My pain was enormous over losing an aunt who had taught me so much about making one's home beautiful and using what you have to make life better. She was also a great example that having a rented house does not mean you cannot care about it. And it always paid off, for her landlords usually ended up *paying her* for her extra care and repair of their rental property—everything within a block radius of where she lived would be clean—and everybody around participated by not throwing down trash, or they had to deal with her (she was a character). The continued pain of my mother going through so many tragic deaths of her loved ones was also painful to watch, but she had so much faith and was so strong. She was my rock and someone I wanted to feel proud of me.

7. My personal experience was rough as a new mother having just had my second child, whom I called our "love child," being that I was not expecting a second baby so soon. (I tease her that *she* had other plans.) The next day after her birth, as I had all my children naturally and at home, came the experience of not being able to walk or move as I lay hanging off the edge of the bed, partially on the wooden floor, not able to make it to the rest room. I lay crying and wet, waiting for my husband to return, as he had just taken my mother home. That was the beginning of my personal, *hardest* trial, being that young and always healthy, never having missed school due to sickness. Here at the age of twenty-one, I was now facing death. The devastating condition left me

helpless for about two months, until that one day I lay unable to take the pain. I did not want to be hospitalized, so the chiropractic doctor had come to see why my legs had given way, but now I could not be touched or hardly moved. I truly found God through this experience.

As illness came over me like a storm of trouble and pain, so I remembered the Bible story about the prophet, and I too made a "deal with God"(or so I thought). He delivered, and I have tried hard to keep my end ever since. He has always kept his, and my experience of "brokenness" has never been from physical disability. But oh how painful the other ways to get the message to me has been, as my journey continues into lessons to be learn. I did learn that I do not need a go-between (like a pastor) to talk directly to the God of the Universe. I usually get a quick response to my prayers.

8. Then came the sudden, senseless death of my sister, whom we loved dearly. She was a kind person, especially as she got older. She was five years older than me, and I was dreaming about her dying the night of her death, only to be awoken to the fact it had happened that very early morning. It was a senseless act, another loved one gone. I realized, with the dream, God had prepared me.

I found that it was better to have one "balanced parent" setting the right examples, setting rules and guidelines with love in the teaching of their child than two broken ones. My sister was the beautiful "tomboy" daughter who loved to follow our daddy (against my mother's wishes) wherever he would go, and many times, the places he went did not prove to be good for her. She also tried to keep up with our two younger brothers, who followed in many ways into our daddy's world. This taught me that I was right in my assessment that the nightlife was not for me.

9. Emotional breakage and spiritual disruptions can be very painful. The spiritual betrayal that erupted into one of my biggest dark nights was when I was falsely accused by a misinformed pastor of starting a rumor about some aberrant sexual behavior happening in the church community. It wasn't a rumor, by the way, and I was neither involved in it nor gossiping about it. His accusation was prejudiced by his friendship with an involved deacon. And then I was faced with the

horror of *dis-fellowship*, without being given due process of a word in my defense. For once, I didn't even attempt to argue; my spirit told me to let go and let God, and it worked. But it was painful. However, truth will always come to light. I passed the test, and more growth came into my life.

10. The death of my mother was a scenario about which she used to prophesy, "One day, one of you will come here and find me dead, and your brother will not even know it."

My oldest brother, who generally stayed in his room reading literature or the Bible, had been with Mother all his life, as he had a disability that was made worse by the incident of being hit in the head with a golf ball at Herman Park. Back then, nobody cared about blacks who got injured on jobs; there was no lawsuit to be thought of. So it resulted in seizures and a nervous condition that would prove to be a challenge for Mother the rest of her life.

The church was a big help, as he would later join the church and grow to be what I call my *Christian monk* brother. To this day, that is what he does: he reads, studies, and listens to Gospel programs. He is the one who rocked me on the porch of Taylor Courts, taught me my times tables and how to drink coffee. Now, and for the last thirty years, I take care of him, being allowed to keep a promise I made to my mother when I was about nine or ten.

I felt as a child that, when my mother passed and if my oldest brother was still living, someone would have to take him in. At ten, I understood that responsibility of who would be a worry on my mother's list; I wanted to relieve her of any unnecessary pain or worry, so I made a promise as a child, which my loving young husband allowed me to keep. And it was not easy in the beginning on us; it was even a "breaking of the spirit" for years, but this too has passed, and it works out as we learn to live and let live. Soon to be eighty, my oldest brother is doing quite well.

But my mother's death happened *as she predicted*, and it taught me how powerful words are. I learned this from her. I also learned that if I could live and cope with my mother's death, I could withstand anything this life had to bring my way, for this would have been my greatest spirit breaker. But then I had to remember I prayed at the age of ten that my mother would be granted the grace to live long enough to see me graduate from high school. I saw her sick too many times and going to the hospital desperately trying to breathe. God was generous with my prayer; she lived long enough to not to just see me graduate, but go to college, get married in the church, and all my three children born and growing old enough to know her, love her, and have good memories of her. So at her wake, how could I complain? I was filled with spiritual gratitude and able to make others feel comfortable to talk and be in peace and joy at her wake and funeral, as she lived for God and fought a hard fight in faith.

These ten experiences were the most major times of broken spirit, occurring in time sequence, but of course there were more. I am sure there will be others that I will have to write about in the future, but for now, ten is my special number for review. Trust me, the mountains and the valleys are always lined up in our lives to strengthen us and produce better *spiritual muscles*. And I am still in the spiritual gym of life, working on my SMs.

I had written three letters one to each of my parents as well as the man who had been in my life as a young person and was very interested in me and would tell everyone he knew that I was his daughter. It was okay when I was young, but as I became an adult, a wife, and a mother, I was not comfortable with what that implied. These letters were very personal and helped me to release the pain that I had inside, hidden by the last words my daddy said to me, "Daddy loves you." After writing a letter to each individually, something strange happened. Every chapter, every poem, every page I typed was in the documents file, except those letters. I have looked and searched all three computers, every digital stick, and nothing.

I had hard copies, though, so I went to have them scanned and placed on a digital stick, and all kinds of weird things happened in my trying to edit or just get them into the book. Then it hit me: I was inspired one morning to write all my feelings, to tell each parent and parental figure what I felt—with respect and with love, but I did not leave any stone unturned. But those letters were for me and them and maybe my family, but they were not to be shared with the world. I have learned when you are on the right path, it flows smoothly, but when things get uneasy, stop, be still, and listen. So the part that kept coming up from the rest, I will share, and it is how the letter begins.

A Letter to My Dear Beloved Mother

> *Dear Mother,*
>
> *This book was ultimately inspired by your ability to weather many storms in your life. They brought you into existence on a special stumbling block that many times became your stepping stone and sometimes your albatross. The one thing you have proved to me is that no matter how hard we try to do what is right, life has a way of showing us how human we can be. You have shown me that, yes, one can teach a valuable lesson, of integrity, honesty, and faithfulness, even though they themselves failed the test on occasions. Hopefully, they would be like you, have a second chance to prove to themselves they could make a difference, as you proved to me the last 19 years of your life being true to your principles. . . .*

The question that changed my life, and renewed my faith confirmed for me that we, even as children, have what we need within us. When I went to Master C. and he answered my question, "Was my daddy my father?" Master C. spoke in a definitive way, as if the words were being whispered into his ears by the spirit that accompanied me to his temple. He does not stutter or look surprised when he channels these communication; he is a spiritual instrument. He said, "The man that was your daddy … is not your father."

I could not do anything but cry softly, because deep inside I knew something was wrong with our relationship. As a child, there was an energy of resistance, but I weathered it, knowing my mother loved me, and the special relationship I had with that secret power of the clouds that I so much talked to as a four-year-old, if not earlier, gave me the strength to not become bitter or victimized. Nor did it paralyze me by the feeling of abandonment of my daddy's affection.

Some may say, "Maybe the monk was wrong in his assessment." I think he was right, being that he knew so much about me *and* my family, without knowing me or even that I was coming. He also predicted the radio job I would get, which I was not even aware of at that time. Much more was predicted, and it all came true. This book is the last part that he predicted, and who would have thought I would be able to tackle such a feat as this book? But it is done.

As much as I would like to say it is a possibility that he was wrong, in my soul I felt it answered the lifelong question, why did Mama love Daddy so? He was a rolling stone, as many black men were in the day, and many men were "stuck" with other men's children. It was a standard joke: Mother's baby ... Father's maybe?

Anyone who knew my mother would never put her in that category, but life is full of surprises, and the one that made this seem so real explains how after my father's death, the man who used to come around once in a while began to come regularly. But the funny thing about it was that my mother could not stand him. Whenever he came, she would leave the room, and he would take me shopping in his Cadillac. He got one every few years or so; sometimes he would take me to see his mother (my grandmother!), and he always beamed with pride as he showed me off. He was kind and generous to me all the time; I just did not feel comfortable with him "lying about me being his child." Once the monk told me my daddy was not my father, I knew who was. And it all made sense: why would my mother, after my daddy's death, allow me to leave the house with a man she could not tolerate, even to sit down and hold a conversation with? Why not stop him from coming if he was not welcome? Because she knew that he was my father, and she knew he would look out for me and provide me with things she could not.

The riddle had been answered.

My daddy had his part that contributed to the events that led to her choices, and yes, she made a choice. The events of his running the streets, drinking, and not providing for his family caused the conditions. She had a choice and found herself in the weak position of many women of the day, and her *mistake* turned out to be much more … *me*. It must have burned her heart and soaked into her spirit, because she hardly ever went anywhere, was always home, cooking, cleaning, and making sure we were cared for the best she could.

I know that God doesn't make mistakes, and neither am I a mistake; my DNA is designed to be what it is for me, and it took two people in the "wrong" to make me happen. My mother was my blessing, and I was her blessing, and later my husband and I were a bigger blessing. He was there to do for her when her own sons were not or could not.

When we were raising our children and finding work during that recession, I bought a life insurance policy for her, and when things got tight in the early eighties, we wrote postdated checks to keep her insurance going. I felt what she had was not enough (and it wasn't), because I did not want her to die and we would have to ask for help to bury her. I had her life insured for five years, and it paid for her funeral, and I was grateful to use every penny, for we put her away the way she deserved. I have kept my promise from the age of ten to care for my older brother; he has been with us for thirty-two years. I don't think her having me was a mistake … do you?

I teach that if you *ask, seek, and knock*, it will be given, answered, and opened. Well, that poem vibrated a question to the universe, and I was sixty-three years old before the answer came to me. I was so ready to receive the truth that has set me free—even as it knocked me down a few notches, as we too had the same issues as many others in our community had. So before anyone judges, be careful.

I was prepared for this news when I struck up a radio-telephone friendship with a radio caller (my respectful friend, I dubbed him Mr. D.). After bringing him on another talk show, he told of his father getting the lady next door pregnant. I thought that was rough, but little did I know I was the result of a similar situation, so therefore be careful how we judge. What I learned from Mr. D. was that family comes with much baggage, and people do what people do. He says there is a way to do wrong *right.* I beg to differ, but I do know what he is saying. He really prepared me for life's possibilities and helped me not to look at everything through my "rose-colored moral glasses" due to my personal self-control and straight-laced practices.

The one secret that many do not know: I have a way of being very observant, as when I saw a tomato plant growing between the cracks in a city sidewalk. When I finally learned that people often just fell into situations, that they were later sorry for, I knew that I was capable of doing anything anyone else could do or had done. The only difference is, knowing this prepares me to watch out, be mindful, and know everyone is innocent of something at one time, before they became guilty. I learned that every time I would say what I would never do something or I did not want something, the universe does not hear *never* or *not,* but hears *want* and *do,* and I end up doing it or wanting it! So, I don't say what "I'll never do …" anymore; instead I say, "As long as I am in my right mind, I will do the right thing."

As Master C. teaches, God loves me, and I shall do no evil. He also says, "Do your duty."

I have my way of saying it by putting the two together and taking out the *no* … "God loves me, and *I do my duty to do good."*

This whole journey has been a blessing: finding out the truth brought me compassion for all three parents and for the many children who are living in a lie. I would hope that we have progressed, that we should not only have birth certificates but DNA certificates—everyone has the medical, legal, and mental right to know who they are from. Men should be able to say Mother's baby and Father's baby *too!*

If this make you uncomfortable, trust me, the truth will set you free, and you can find comfort in knowing who you really are, as far as your human side goes.

We can also know, if we choose to, who we are on the spirit side. This is my story, and I was told to tell it. I hope my honesty in sharing my truth will help some *tell* the truth or *find* the truth. This is not one of those confessions of someone who "hated" or was upset with their mother; I loved my mother with all my heart and still do. I would live through this again if that was the only way I could have her as my mother.

True love, some hurt to hear, but it does not hurt to bear.

—AF

Concept of Healing and the Healing Process

Starting this section, a definition for healing is a must. I have asked many people to describe the meaning of a broken spirit, and I have also asked what are the parts of the healing process. Many people who have submitted their definitions of a broken spirit have also offered a solution at the same time. This chapter is important, because we need to feel the importance of knowing that if God is Love then that love is unconditional. There are laws of the universe that are in order just as the sun rises and the sun sets in the same two locations every day. That is one of the ways we know God is the same yesterday and tomorrow. In this chapter, I will name some of these "laws of the universe." Another way to think of God is as the Universe, as many of us have been taught that God is the beginning and the end, the Alpha and the Omega, which also describes the universe. Some prefer to call that great and powerful source *God*.

There are many names that God is called, and out of respect for all who may be reading this book, it is no secret that I have been a Christian most of my life. But it has not been "boxed" in the normal traditions of Christianity. When I was ten, my father was tragically killed and my mother sought refuge and help with five children, looking to the traditional church. One included a Baptist minister who told my youngest older sister, who was fifteen at the time and needed shoes, "I cannot take the church money and buy you shoes; you do not attend our church." To say the least, it left a bad taste in all of our mouths to hear this from *my father's brother,* who had come to Houston poor and needing work and became a preacher. His church labeled and dismissed people like my dad, who "drank and ran the streets," as a sinner.

This was a family conversation we had many times: I remember visiting my uncle the minister on several occasions. My mother prepared us by saying if anyone wanted to know anything about our father to say, "I don't know, ma'am (or *sir*)." Whether they asked what we had for dinner or "Did your father come home last night?" the answer was "I don't know." There was a joke about all of us—we were the "I don't know" children.

Unlike my other siblings, I would talk to my elders, whom I felt I could trust. Even as a child I had a sense of trust in people. It kept me safe mostly, and a few times in got me in a little trouble. But overall, it worked for me, so I became the communicator of the family, which paid off. At the early age of twelve, I had to communicate with landlords, pastors, and even public lawyers, for my mother was often sick with asthma (which always seemed to occur when "trouble" came). I have never been intimidated by people with power, money, or education; I have always felt that they were no better than me and neither was I any better than them. They might have skills or information that I might not have, but I knew and had some things that they may have lacked also. Time, people, places, and circumstances are all a part of our makeup. Looking back, I can see the plan God had for me.

My mind always goes back to this tomato I saw growing on a wiry one-stem vine between the separation in a sidewalk, in Southern California, on the campus of a college. I was about thirty at the time, and I videotaped it; and it has never left my mind. Anytime I hear of reasons I or anyone could not achieve something, this lonely plant comes to mind. The odds of people walking around this one stem growing tall enough to produce a tomato tells me a different story: that tomato could not have grown there without the consciousness of many people to *not* step on it, to *not* pull it up, and to *not* just cut it off in its growth process. For an actual tomato to be on it, meant the environment in which it grew, even though it did not belong, *allowed* it to survive. I am sure at some point the yard man or someone must have seen it as just a weed, in the first stages of growth … but it was given a chance.

Those who believe in divine purpose may look at this tomato plant in even another light. The purpose of this plant was to bear a tomato, and as it grew, showing up in the "wrong place"(between the harsh slabs of concrete rather than an intentional garden), the universe protected it from the running, walking, and the interference of any object (leaf blowers, edgers, clippers, cars!) that could have caused destruction to its growth. So actual *incidents* had to take place that caused the plant to be spared. Until one day, some probably noticed the budding vine and wanted to see the outcome, so they started to purposely let it "do its thing," until the results of its purpose was exposed for all to see: the beauty of allowing what some may have seen as a weed grow into something wonderful. I am sure the *law of vibration* helped many times, as there may have been those who would have destroyed it on purpose, but it was not in their vibrational path, and so it was able to escape their wrath.

That tomato plant, reminds me of myself and others who grew up in Fifth Ward, Texas. I have been allowed to be in some of the most beautiful homes in our community, with full trust in my credibility not to steal or destroy the environment. As I have mentioned, my experience as a child of taking a face towel from someone who trusted me left me horrified and embarrassed, but it was a *hypnotic rhythm* moment at the age of eleven. To this day, I love buying towels as gifts for people *and* receiving them. As a child, a nice towel was a luxury. As an adult, one of the reasons hotels do not have to worry about me *stealing* their towels is I usually bring one of my own.

Yes, *I see this tomato as me*, simply because of how I grew up. There were people supporting me, nourishing me with information, knowledge, and wisdom, *allowing* me to grow under their care, though I was not "supposed" to be there, and even sending me home many times with pans of food. This is an example of the *universal law of allowing.* It is one of the universal laws that helped me grow up with wisdom and develop integrity at an early age. That integrity paid off many times, during school and later in life, and it still works today.

While attending junior high school—this particular school started in the sixth grade—there was a girl whom I had met before my father was killed. Her older sister lived across from my aunt (my mother's sister), and we met up in school. I was so glad to see somebody that I knew, and we became close friends. One day that friendship ended. She asked me to hold a purse she had found, until she got back. I stood by the bathroom door waiting for her to come back, and within a few minutes, I began to hear some noise. As she came closer, another girl, looking scared and upset, was crying that her purse was missing—someone had stolen it out of the bathroom. The principal was behind the two of them, and as they approached me, my friend said loudly,

"You can search me! I do not have that girl's purse!" I could feel the blood rush to my face as I stood frozen by the door. I understood now why she gave me the purse to hold. She had stolen the purse and wanted to hide it, so she selected me. Afraid of being caught up in something that I would not like to be involved in, I stepped up forward and said, "Is this your purse?" as I held up the small bag. The principal took the purse, had the young lady check it—nothing was missing—and spoke to my friend and me in a voice of disappointment. In the principal's office, I learned several lessons, one about *blind trust* and another about *true sorrow.*

The principal asked, "Which one of you took the purse?"

My friend then began to "throw me under the bus," as they would say in today's slang. She said quickly and with an attitude, "I do not have the purse."

This, to me, meant whoever had the purse stole the purse. I did not steal the purse, but I had it! I explained to the principal what had happened, as tears began to roll down my eyes. I was still going through the pain and the loneliness of my father's death, and my family was so disjointed, not even having a home of our own—but I was not a thief. I had worked in the homes of many neighbors and never touched their purses or any money lying around. My friend now became my "friend-enemy."

She turned on me and denied that she gave me the purse. It was my word against hers. The difference was I truly was afraid and sorry about this situation I found myself in. The principal knew that I was new, and he knew from teachers of my character, and excused me as he turned to my new "friend-enemy," and said, "Your attitude is one of anger and hostility, and you are lying. You show no humility about what has happened here today." He opened the door for me. I thanked the principal and rushed out, thankful for having the sense to be nonaggressive in being accused. And so, the truth was revealed.

The second lesson was about having good character, humility, and respect for those who are in authority over you. My mother taught all of us that—even my brothers, who were in and out of trouble; they always were respectful to those in charge. It made their incarceration less difficult, and at least they came out of the system with the best record in character. No matter where you find yourself, be on your best behavior!

The temporary fear for me was to never be on the wrong side of the law. And this purse situation was a great scare for me.

The third lesson was be careful who you trust. I should have asked questions about something that should not have been my problem. Why *couldn't* she hold on to the purse herself? I now get more clear about why I do what I do when asked by someone else, especially when they are capable of doing it for themselves: why would anyone ask you to hold a purse without a good reason?

Lesson learned and scars earned.

—AF

6ft. Companion Art
Imhotep and Akua
BLCC ..by Akua

A Different Way to Love

My mother grew up without her mother. She lacked the kisses and hugs that her mother could not give.
It was different for her to manage after her mother's death while pregnant with twins, who also did not live.
She grew up wanting to go to school and be someone really great. She was smart, but in those days, girls didn't wait to marry late.
My mother was without a mother to love her and keep her safe and warm.
She met my father-to-be, who promised to keep her from harm. She didn't know how to be affectionate with hugs and kisses on our cheeks.
She loved us so greatly, I felt it through the many little things she did week after week.
She washed our clothes with her hands. She sewed and made them too.
She cooked whatever there was. Groceries, there were few. She took care of our cuts, colds, and flu. Mother was always home to do what she could do.
Sometimes when she was sick and could hardly breathe,
She'd bend over the kitchen sink, refusing to give up and leave.
While sitting between her beautifully shaped legs,
I'd be getting my hair combed. She saved money on hair conditioner made with vinegar and eggs.
Every day when I came in from school, she'd be waiting at the door.
I could smell the fresh cornbread, and I always begged for more.
We sat and drank coffee, as I matured in a different kind of way. I sat with Mother and listened to the wise things that she would have to say.
My mother taught me how to live and have the right kind of pride.

Suggestion:

Enjoy memories of your loved ones by the things you do to make life better now. Sometimes things that cost the least are the things best-remembered, like sitting down and giving time to each other, sharing that special cup of coffee or tea that adds the warmth and fragrance that gives a memory its staying power, because whenever the aroma is smelled, the memory will be renewed.

A *Grave* Situation Causes a Broken Spirit for Many

I am so grateful for the many people who have added color to my life, please know that I would name each and every one of you, but I will include those whom I may have missed and those for whom there was not enough space in this edition when I do *Healing of a Broken Spirit II.* But I must give thanks to one person who, over twenty years ago, helped me at one of my Broken Spirit situations.

My mother was buried in a cemetery on the outskirts of town. It became one of my first advocate issues in the community—her grave could not be found, because she was one among many African Americans who had either been buried on top of one another or their remains destroyed (probably fire but not fire as in *cremation*). It was broadcast on TV, with me walking through where my mother's remains should have been put to rest—by the fig tree and the pecan tree. I could not believe even after death my mother could not find a resting spot, whether her remains were part of *her* or not; respect for the dead's remains should be carried out as paid for. Others joined in with the same complaints, and the owner of the cemetery had charges filed against him for the horrible crime against bodily remains. But really, the crime is against the grieving families.

I was going on-air about the issue on Magic 102 when I got to the station and found out I was to be going on at nine at *night* not in the morning. Leroy Patterson was on the air and was expecting a guest, but it was raining and the guest had not arrived, so he allowed me to come onto his show. I truly came "from out of the blue"; he did not know me.

But he allowed me to address my mother's lost remains, on the air. I was forever grateful to him and met his lovely wife. They became good friends of mine, and when he developed cancer, I wrote a poem for him, that he said would go in his book, to finish his life. He was known, later in life before he passed, as Ambaksye Jarbari a great radio personality who was respected by the community,

Last but not least, Bernard Thibodaux writer for the Forward Times Newspaper, wrote the first newspaper article of me as Business Person of the Week, where the beautiful outfit my sister LaVera, designed for me was worn.

Lying, One of the Things God Hates

Does lying disconnect us from God?

At one time or another, everyone lies—on purpose or lie because of *fear* or a *mistake.* Some feel *forced* to lie to protect themselves in certain situations—such as to get or keep a job or lying to their parents, or to any one with authority over them, who gives them orders that you must follow or give up your livelihood. Thus comes the choice to act for character over comfort or even sometimes survival.

God judges the heart; therefore the intent is
more important than the content.

—AF

When and why do you lie? Only you can make an assessment of that question. It is important that we each answer that question for ourselves and look to see, whenever we feel a "disconnect from God," if lying was somewhere within the context of the situation. Sometimes we lie to ourselves, to convince ourselves to go against the grain of positivity or to go with the flow of negativity—at times the negativity flow is more acceptable and without much effort. Thus, going along to get along.

There are times we feel lying is saving a person from harm. Thus is the intent worth the lying if the purpose is to do good? This is a question of the heart, the mind, and the soul. This is where the *in*tent could outweigh the *con*tent. It is still a lie, but one would think it might be justified to withhold information that could cause a person to be physically harmed. However, in true life, this is not the case when most people lie, and that is a call for judgment that one must make for the greater good.

The Everyday Liar

The everyday liar is the one who truly must feel a disconnect, and often. The daily liar is one who frequently lies for acceptance, to be noticed, to cover up inferiority, and many times, out of jealousy, to deflate someone who he or she feels is getting too much praise. Lying is like smoking, drinking, or any habit that is practiced daily: it becomes addictive, and many liars become habitual liars. If it flows with ease and without discomfort, this is the liar most dangerous in his ability to be smooth and convincing.

We all need to face the lies in our life and understand that to willfully lie and to do so to do harm or deceive for gain and destruction is a *direct* disconnect from Spirit.

L lacking in self-confidence

Y yearning for approval

I insecure and in need

N needing to be needed

G getting something for nothing

The Love of a Mother

Her love lives on forever; it never dies.
Her love grows and softly multiplies.
Her children are the footprints
She leaves to carry on.
So do great things to honor her;
She really is not gone.
For her spirit is always with you,
Protects you day by day.
Your mother is your Angel
Who protects you in every way.
Your mother has left you
A gift for you to see.
Just look in the mirror,
And that is where she will be.
For you are a reminder
Of the love she left behind.
Her love will go on as your children
Go through time.

The One Who

To my oldest brother, who bypasses a broken spirit, on his 80th birthday

My childhood was quite much to do,
As I look back and think of the one who …
The one who rocked me on the front porch many times,
The one who taught me my times tables to sharpen my mind,
The one who would sometimes hide
His giant Babe Ruth candy bar—he had a little stingy side—
The one who taught me how to drink my coffee black,
The one who I knew (and still do) had my back,
The one who showed me how to play golf in the backyard,
My brother Isaac, who showed me how to live for God.
He is unique, he is funny, and he sometimes says what is on his mind.
One thing we all know: serving God is his life, full time.

First Third Love Pencil sketch of Grandson
by Akua

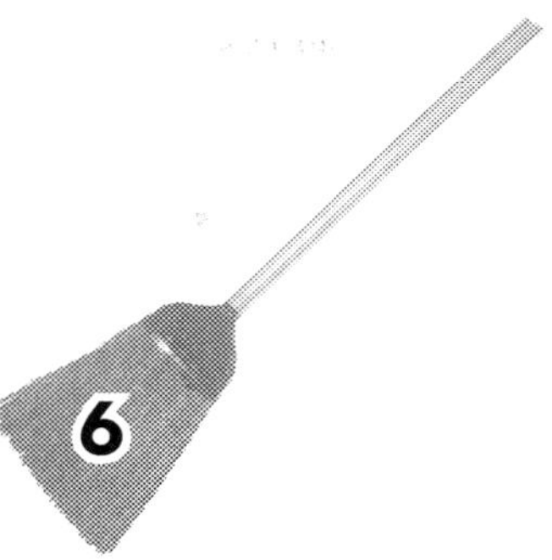

6

The Law of Attraction at Work

Did you know that our thinking creates and bring to us what we think about?

All our lives are a summation of what we want, what we do, and what we think about. This is how the *law of attraction* works. It does not matter who you are; you are given the same physical laws of the universe to provide for you, by the choices you make, the decisions you decide, and also the company you keep.

Whatever your interest is, if you pursue it, it will multiply. Many times, we are not patient enough to wait for quality, and we accept whatever comes our way. This can be a good thing—as in being grateful for a little; one day it will grow to be more—but we still should consider quality when the situation is not life or death.

For example: "I need a good leather purse." Patience and planning can bring you what you want and the quality that you want. But what if, in your haste, you decide to buy a knock-off purse? It *looks* like leather, *feels* like leather, but it does not hold up, so the money—which may have been only 30 percent of what a real leather purse would have cost—is now lost money, for you still need a purse. Impatience led you to get a purse just for the looks, but it also speaks to the *ego*.

I use the purse example, because many people spend huge amounts of money for designer names and don't get quality, and many times, the purse *cost* more money than it will ever carry. One day, you look in your closet and you have thirty or forty purses! You *attracted* them by your choices—of sales, deals, and even gifts. The same analogy applies to anything in life that we wish to have. With intent, constant thought, words of "I will," "when I do," "I am," and so on, we can bring much into our lives. Why not use this law to bring love, knowledge, good health, and wealth that is based on the ability to have and share in balance and harmony? Of course, a good purse can be a great asset too!.

What Is Healing?

Healing is a way to connect one's self to become whole. A way to heal is a reconnecting to what caused our lives to malfunction and brought us to dis-ease (disease) in the first place. Healing is a way to prevent that disconnection from occurring.

One gift my mother gave to me was her way of explaining my introduction to the world of Fifth Ward, Texas. She said her doctor told her that I was "the healthiest baby the doctor had seen in a long time."

That simple, positive statement has stayed with me all my life, making me fearless about helping others who just might be down with illness and that most people might fear or refuse to be near.

It has also made me feel that no illness would have power over me. Whenever I remember this statement, for some reason it gives me a boost of energy! This is one example of words staying with a person, and just like good words can stay, for some reason bad words seem to stick even harder.

What Is Spirit?

Consider "problems" that come in a character clothed in hate, jealousy, fault-finding, judging, envy, guilt, anger, or egotism. When you see the words *broken spirit,* know that it is a *synonym* for being separated from God in our mind and heart, which causes a disconnect.

The worst thing in my life has always held the best beginnings for my life to be renewed. *All good comes from God.* But when we disconnect from God, we then allow our minds to feed on negativity, because it is disconnected from faith, peace, love, and truth.

Spirit is so vast and wide and also pinpointed in the essence of your being. To me, it is the *being* part of our human-being. I want to develop more of my *being* and so enhance my *humanism*. The very part of the Great Creator is the spirit of divinity.

The Three Sisters Aired on PBS Special
By Akua

A Healing Spirit

Three Sisters

My Trade Mark

Akua Fayette's Three Sisters

"On their knees with a book"

Wrapped Heads

Their heads are wrapped, for it is not important what the length, texture,color, or style of the hair…what is important, is what's in the mind, the heart and how we treat one another.

Shoulder to shoulder

They are shoulder to shoulder, because they lean on one another for support (spiritually, emotionally,physically and economically).

Kneeling

As they kneel, which can be spiritual, but also a way to nurture their

children, through correction with love, by
looking into their eyes with this love,

and seeing their pain and their passion, leaves no desire to abuse.

A Book

They share one book, Goose Sense,(it could be any book
of value of wisdom) because they are on the same

page of life. They are like the geese, they (The Three Sisters)

nurture and care for the community.

Reading is a very important part of their culture.

Black Skin

They are jet black which holds all colors from the blackest

to the whitest, for they stand for all

humanity, YOU could be a "Three Sister."

This gives me the opportunity to "Spot Light"

(As Dr. J Walls would say Spot Light)

"The Three Sisters".

These three Women have crossed my life and many others.

I am giving them honors in this book, for I know them personally. They've experienced many broken spirits over their life time. Each of them would be in the category of an elder.

Many of us look up to them

as a Mother figure.

I have met many people with a healing spirit. In other words, they are positive and full of sage wisdom. **Dr. Edith Irby Jones** is one of these people. From the first time I had the pleasure of meeting her and attending many of her birthday parties, given by her daughter Myra Jones Romaine.

I was sad to have missed Dr. Edith I. Jones's eighty-seventh birthday this year. For the first birthday that I attended of hers, I painted one of my "Soul Wooden Bowls," portraying the symbolism of her interesting and successful life. She loved it, as she loves art. I am in honor of her living legacy, publishing this poem that I wrote for her … it explains how she was the only black student in her medical school, and the first in Arkansas.

She has been given so many awards, but I felt my bowl could stand for her successful life in medicine and community service. Her life story tells about how black servants in the school brought her a flower a day to remind her they were "praying and looking out for her," even though they could not express their concerns out loud, for the school was still segregated—she could not eat in the cafeteria with her white classmates!

Words Unspoken
By Akua Fayette

As the days were full of eyes
Watching the young black girl
As she moved down the hall, surrounded by
The "whiteness" of her day,
Not giving in,
Not giving up,
Standing tall,
Gently smelling the flower of the day.
The rich smell of blackness through the fragrance of words unspoken

History:
In 1958, Edith Irby Jones broke the racial barriers of southern medical schools when she became the first Black person, male or female, admitted to the University of Arkansas School of Medicine. In 1958, Jones became the first woman president of the National Medical Association, a predominantly Black medical society.

Black Women In America, page 927
By: D,Hine, E. Brown & R .Penn

Upon contacting Dr. Jones, within a minute, she was dictating to me her definition of a broken spirit. She has lived her life so well, serving and getting her work done, she only had to start talking, and I wrote. I see why she has been so successful.

So I went straight to work on this book. Every time I see her, she has a positive attitude and a smile.

Please look up her rich history. She is a well-kept secret in Texas, but known around the world.

Jean Wilkins Dember MHS

Jean Wilkins Dember, MHS, is well known and respected for her indomitable and persistent struggles against racism/colorism, especially within the Catholic Church. Usually working behind the scenes, she has fomented important changes in Mental Health arenas all over the United States. She founded the organization, Afrikans United For Sanity Now, which has received many awards for combatting inequities against people of color down through the years... Zoom Info

A Legacy in Motion

By Akua Fayette

Mother Dember sometimes called the Button Lady,
She walks among the rich, the poor, and the shady.
Having met Mother Dember before her fame,
I have seen her fervor and passion remain.
She walks in the shoes that no one else can fill.
She is a legacy in motion, and her life is not guided by pills.
She walks the talk that she preaches like a "historical goddess" in her button- filled garb.
She gives the Catholic Church much to think about, and it is not all about God.
Whether it is a wedding or a funeral, she doesn't put away her *sign.
She stands firm and strong as her buttons grow with time.
She is a walking history board, and she lives it every day.
I recently spent three hours with her ... and her sign was set to stay!

Harriet Tubman, Sojourner Truth, to name a few, is the company she would run with by the things she chooses to do.

Her life is dimensional, as she believes in the Whole of mankind.

She watches what she consumes, with spiritual knowledge on her mind.

I am so grateful to not only know her, but to be a friend indeed.

She has planted the seed of the illness of racism, and our minds need to be freed.

One thing I know she will be known for … is her knowledge of the colon, and she reminds us to forget not …

When we begin to clean out our colons, it will help to clean out our minds!

Health is very important and it is the urgency of our Times.

Mother Dember carries a sign with her wherever she goes. It talks about brutality and other injustices

Photo of Mother Dember's Hat by Akua

Mary Etta Berry Delaney

October 12 1923 born to Melvin and V.L. Berry in a little town in East Texas, they named her Mary Etta. Mary having been married twice the mother of six children, three children for each marriage. She was employed by Houston Independence School District for 38 years. At the age of 75, she enrolled in Harris County Community College.

She was granted her Angel Wings on October 7, 2011

This is a tribute to
The Late Mama Delaney
Who gave me encouragement and examples of never giving up!

Mama Delaney

Living life and loving all that it has to offer.
Being called "Mama" is a compliment from the Universe
of Understanding Love and "Hard-knocks"
That's why I will always love my "Mama

The late Mama Delaney

I am giving her flowers now, but I also gave her fresh flowers for the last three days before she transition. Her best friend and my mentor, Mother Dember and I was at her home by her side to the end. I truly witnessed the peace that comes over a body when pain, grief and sickness are overcome by the spirit departing from the fleshly garments. I recited a poem I wrote for her at her funeral it tells of her strength, love and community service. She was catching the bus while into her eighties to help others, she paid the way for many children to go to Georgia on SHAPE Community Center's Youth History Tour during the summer to Georgia and she also attended with them. She loved children and gave of her time and money to help them any way she could.

Crabs in a Basket
First and Last art about the negative system

Crawling out of the Basket and Dragging the Rope Behind

I once painted a picture depicting a basket of crabs wearing all kinds of ethnic clothing, symbolizing that a "crab mentally" is not just for people who aren't educated culturally. Many who are at the top of the holders of cultural information have that same mentality—wanting to pull down anyone about to transcend the holding cell of the bucket. It is the thinking of a man who oozes his hate not his skin color or his clothes. Having always wanted to carry someone *with* me as I went up any "ladder of positive direction," it is one of my personal pet peeves that some people think "the proverbial pie is not big enough."

When I wrote my first book, a wonderful young man did the art. I insisted, even though I could do my own art, that I was not an illustrator. Therefore, I wanted to share the rewards of a bestselling children's book series with a person who desired to be an illustrator. So I found a young man who did, and I explained the pay would come as we published the book. It was my vision, and it still is. He did a great job, but as soon as I did the first batch, he came to me at the instruction of "friends," saying we needed three or more lawyers, and that I could not use his images of the geese without his permission. He was a nice young man but had no vision and bad counsel. I wanted him to be known and had allowed him to sign his signature on every page, so people would know the art was not mine and belonged to him, giving him name recognition. I could not at the time afford him and three or more attorneys, nor did I want to tie myself to a contract where my creation was not mine to use as I wanted and when I wanted. The self-publication of *Goose Sen*se was very successful, and I will be soon taking it and the other books in the series, as yet unpublished, to a new level.

I had the pleasure of meeting him again recently—this time as a young father who told me he knew he'd made a mistake. I assured him I did not take it personally; he just did not understand and was given advice that did not help him.

I could write of a number of times trying to include others in my travels out of the "crab basket." It sometimes seemed like sabotage or someone taking over an idea and running with it elsewhere. This book is not just about the many experiences that I learned my lessons from, being knocked down, overlooked, misunderstood, and at fault many times myself, but it's also about always working out of passion and principle, which is not always right, but it's usually with good intentions.

This book is giving me the opportunity to give back and allow some who would never write a book or get the opportunity to see their words or names in print. I had the pleasure once of seeing my name in the appreciation page of a book that I believe will one day become a movie, as she is an excellent writer. In the same way, I am hoping to share the experience of having one's thoughts or ideas published, here in the form of a definition or an opportunity to encourage others to except their religious concepts about spirits and brokenness.

Some of the writers included here are also the people who have helped me in different ways, though some ways have yet to be revealed to me. But each one has a purpose for us to have crossed each other's paths. Some chose to add extra information, some wanted to share their ability in poetry. As long as the editor or publisher had no problem with the entries, I was willing to give them a chance to get their words, names, or info. out. This is my gift.

This book is dealing with the *brokenness* that I encountered on my journey, and I want you to know how the truth can set you free, even though it hurts like something awful!

Definitions of Healing a Broken Spirit

The following definitions are from people who have come from all walks of life at a well-known community center called SHAPE (Self-Help for African People through Education). Most are elders—who could know better about broken spirits?

I recall one lady saying, "I'm writing a book myself, so I won't participate with anyone's book, 'because I'm writing about *my* life." I wish she had considered that participating wasn't about giving me information to write a book. Trust me, I have much more to write, and Book II is on the way. But I feel she lost an opportunity to help someone else, maybe even herself, for many who participated said it was enlightening to explore what I'd asked them to, and they found some things about themselves they needed to heal.

Here Are a Few from SHAPE

To merely exist,
To succumb to an earthly master,
Be it the master drugs, sex, or a person ...
Defines that your spirit has been broken.

—D. Parker

Life's up and downs, the choices we make, the consequences, the loss of hope, the company we keep ... that mean us no good, and time moves fast and time moves fast as we look back and see time ... wasted.

—K. Morgan

The spirit is broken for certain reasons; it is important for our success to understand the spirit of God.

—P. Anderson

A spirit of "Woe is me, what am I going to do with my life?" Well, I am glad you asked that ... That is a good thing, and Jesus has the answer, and you don't need to have a spirit of brokenness ... Jesus has the answer ... So I recommend Jesus as the answer.

—B. Scott

Dear Mother Dember.

I am so honored to respond to your last two letters, and want you to know I have your first letter.

You wrote me over 15 or more years ago, and I have some flyers from my first time meeting you, so I do not ever want to be called out for not responding to your letters. (smile) I love receiving your letters and feel humbled by your precious time that you give when you write these letters by hand. I do not want you to suffer through my handwriting, for when I get going my handwriting becomes unreadable (smile), and I don't want to take up your time in "handwriting translation." (Smile)

I have learned so much from your steadfastness, and you have shared your deepest desire to have the mental illness of our people resolved through the study and the testing to be provided for racism, especially among those that have control over our lives such as policemen, judges, teachers, mentors, etc.

You are definitely on-purpose, and your rewards will be great for your sacrifice ... I want to continue your legacy throughout my art and my writings.

You have inspired me to put more energy in the healing of our people, I am putting this in my intention of the Universe to go toward that reversal of hate to love.

It really is about fear, for a people who jumped off mountains, jumped over hills, dove in the deepest waters, went into the farthest part of the atmosphere, and into the darkest part of the forest ... these people are truly a fearful people ... funny right?

Fear is opposite of love, and for those who do not like us and we them ... it is fear.

I do not hate them or anyone ... therefore I do not fear them.

Their fear of our going forward is so grand in mental position, that to see us become more confused by trying to imitate their worst habits … (Learn not the ways of the Heathen).

I am on a journey in part because of you; I choose to do it in the way I have been "called" to do it … you are a great example of not being concerned what people think.

I do not stand out as a singer, but I once sang a song because I had to face my fear of singing in public … I did it and I don't have to repeat it (smile).

I recall on the inauguration of our first Black Mayor … that you stood up alone and began to sing the Negro National Anthem … of course I stood next to you and began to join in, thanks to facing prior fear and respect for my elders … I was not going to let you do it alone … even if only the two of us stood among thousands and sang at the top of our lungs (you of course were louder than me (smile) …

I will be speaking to someone on your behalf, about a subject that needs to be addressed … having community respect and the council of our Wise-Elders.

One thing I want to say is that I will be doing a part II of Healing a Broken Spirit. *Part II leads to leadership, and will be featuring the people in the community who want to tell their story, because I believe nearly all the organizations have come out of a "brokenness of some kind," and there are stories to be told in Unity. For once, I want to bring my people together and I believe this book can help to do that. My Intention is to show how adversity can bring on "universities of thought and goodwill."*

I have had many offers to finish my formal education, but when I see what it brings about in the world, I realize that my journey is a special education, and for what I need to do to be grounded, my PHD—and years of experience and more to come, for we never finished learning if we are "well-learned." I met one person who proudly claimed a PhD but said there was nothing anyone could teach him, he was through with being talked to and taught.

I believe you are forever open to learning, as we understand that our system of education has failed us … Of all people, we should know better to not close the door of learning.

I had an ah-ha moment when I read the article about the melanin … and the connection to the spirit-imparting life … the first contact to life (spirit) is next to blackness: melanin.

This drew me back to a Bible verse, which states "to much is given, Much more is required." … Is this possibly why we are able to be so dishonored and abused and yet we are still, by far, loving and forgiving people by nature? Our biggest unsolved situation *(I no longer call problems …* problems) … *which starts between our ears, in our minds, because it is how we look at what I call "unsolved situations" for deep inside, we have the answers to our situation. We just need to reconnect with that source of energy that is inside of us. As a people, we have disconnected from our Spiritual roots … This is my personal observation, as in the last four years, I have been "low key" and rarely interactive with the whole community, but instead a selective part, which does not mean that my love has lessened for the community that I served, although I live elsewhere, but it was time for me to take care of "home," my residential community and be able to use the talents and the abilities that had been "placed on hold," as I was in a Sit Be Still and know that I am God "valley."*

I see you in the trenches every day as a warrior against racism, and I want to have your back on my end as a patron of love with the ability to help heal the wounds of fear and hurt, which I feel will help end racism as we know it—for all racism, in my mind, is their problem not just our problem—with the spiritual ability to reconnect that "Energy Source" called love, which we know as God.

I would love to talk to you about a solution to put to work in starting the ball rolling … on Healing the Illness of Racism … which is the fear of a culture evolved into hate.

Truly Yours,
Akua Fayette
*PLHW**

☕ ☕ ☕

Broken Spirits come in all scenarios. Could the justice system be part of breaking spirits? Here is an interesting perspective of justice … or rather, *injustice.*

> We all start at the starting line of life, with evenly distributed seasoning of spirit—dignity, integrity, respect, etc.
>
> Therefore, no one is better than another.
>
> Then *Society*, the villain/hero, enters that we the people have to encounter as life goes on. At this intersection, making intelligent decisions and moves are critical to enhance the *spirit* or to succumb to *Society.*
>
> One thing that provokes my broken spirit, which I find repugnant, is to stand under duress, when a judge enters and leaves the courtroom. *We the people and the judge have equal seasoning.*
>
> Moreover, I see a lake of humanity languishing under the Pearce Elevated, whose seasoning is more deflated than my previous reference. Homelessness and hopelessness are profound Houston Downtown making an indelible reality show into our psyche.
>
> —Ms. Howard

* My mantra, *peace, love, health, and wealth.*

My Spirit is broken when I think that everything must be perfect, and that I must be wrong about something most of the time. Then I become fearful and react out of fear and become paralyzed. It is healed when I realized that being is enough, just being, and doing what works for right now. I am okay when I am doing my best at being me without fear.

—Anonymous

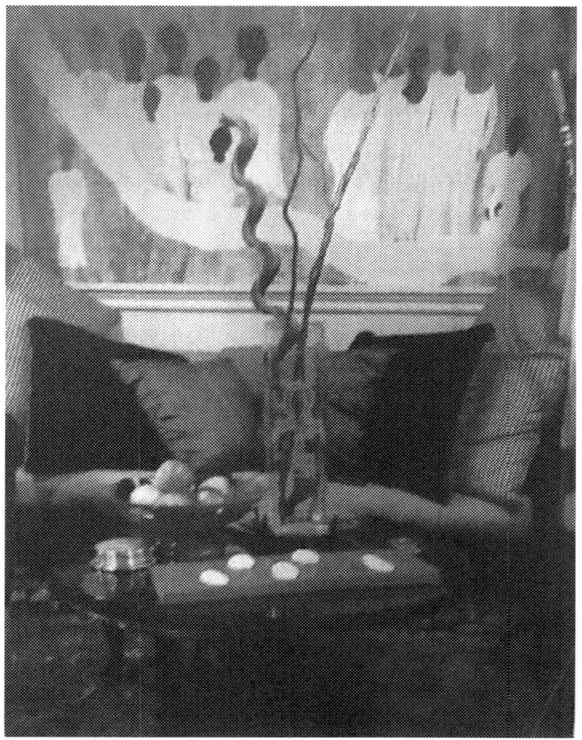

Beginning of family wall mural by Akua

Remember the Song … "On the *Road* Again"?

For Smooth Flowing:

Remembering
Only
Appreciation
Daily

I am really learning, how much I am responsible for my happiness, which leads into my inner joy. I use driving as an analogy for how my life can be, what it is meant to be. I am responsible for my health, wealth, and my peace, which all leads to great inner joy.

Where I end up in life is where I have driven myself, be it by right or left turns, be it by stopping or going, or sometimes just going in circles. It is my journey, and I have the steering under my control, unless I give it over to someone who takes me where *they* want me to go—and to be honest, that does not happen anymore, hardly ever. I am driven by my beliefs and my desire to make my trip the best trip of this life, customized just for me.

Let's go for a ride with Akua; she is the one who has driven the shortest distance but the most fulfilled itinerary. She has received more bang for her bucks while the "younger me" paid the price for the trip now called *smooth flowing.*

- "On the Road Again" is about not just finding one's PATH (personal acceptance to heaven), but it is about *staying on that path.*
- There are signs that we must recognize, to help us know or monitor when we veer off the PATH.
- Our emotions—fear, hate, anger, jealousy, frustration, stress, headaches, backaches, and pains out of nowhere—can be the signals we need to get back on the road.

I use the *gravel,* the dirt, and the ditch as the symbols to represent our emotions of inner-happy decliners. In other words, they take our joy, our peace, and eventually our health away from us. And many times, this leads to premature departure from our bodies. The spirit that is housed in these bodies, to get the different jobs done here on earth in our limited time and space as human beings, exits when we run too far off the road. It's like while driving, when we hit that annoying bumpiness from leaving the road for even just a few inches—it is the first warning that we are going off-course. The gravel can be identified as something small, like an annoyance when we agree to something that we do not want to do; then we begin to complain about being involved. Or it can be feeling bad about a lie that you told or that you went along with so that you *wouldn't* get involved or hurt someone's feelings.

What about a lack of joy for someone's good fortune ... that you thought should have been yours? Being that crab in the bucket. Remember the last time you allowed your mind to wander into the past of un-forgiveness and found a tinge of depression, -anger, or despair?

Once you continue on the gravel and begin to go even farther, it gets a little easier, but it can provide a false sense of safety. The kind of safety in finding someone with the same gripes and complaints that you have. Or sizing up someone else in comparison and feeling like you are justified in your attitude of negativity and unhappiness.

This trip has moved to the level of danger when you begin to go farther into the false safety zone ... and find yourself in the ditch or a hung up on a concrete embankment! The trip now will either be delayed or postponed until "repairs" can be made to your "mode of transportation."

But maybe you were lucky and *noticed* the ditch or the embankment and took a quick detour just in time. It only caused your trip to be delayed until you could reconnect, after going miles out of the way, till you could make a *spiritual* U-turn.

What will your mindset be by the time you make that turnaround?

Will you have made the assessment that because of the choices you made, the trip hit a few stops, interruptions, bad bumps, and you got an uncomfortable ride? And of course you might have, along the way, picked up a few "hitchhikers," for good or ill. Of those who didn't scare you or threaten your way back to your connection, you may have surely saved them from further harm in their own lives.

This is the opportune time to assess the ups and the downs of the trip so far and how the rest of this journey could profit you—and possibly others—by what you have learned. One of the important things to remember is it is not what you want *others* to do to make your journey better, but what you have learned to finish the trip, taking full responsibility.

1. Keep your eyes on the road.
2. Respect the gravel shoulder as a mild warning.
3. Pull over; sit, be still, and figure out where you are going.
4. Giving a ride or a lift is great as long as you use wisdom in whom you pick up, so that *you* reach your desired destination.
5. The best safety check is to be focused and on course.
6. Leave unnecessary baggage behind (things and sometimes people).
7. Appreciate your "vehicle" (maintain your body, mind, and spirit for safety).
8. Keep your windshield free of cracks and debris (smile!).
9. Stay on the road, and *be happy.*

And remember to keep a check on the "battery," your source of energy and creativity. You don't want a "disconnect"; it could delay your journey for a few minutes or for a lifetime ... the choice is up to you!

The New Year—a New Start

A new year, a new you!

My practice over the last ten years has been to paint the old year out and the new year in. This year, there were far too many gun shots ringing in the air, and my mind and my responsibility had been on writing only. So this time, I *wrote* the old year out and the new year in!

I then began to read a letter by someone whom I admire, someone that I recognize as our modern-day Harriet Tubman and Sojourner Truth combined. Truth be known, she is our own Mother Dember (Mother D.), a one-of-a-kind of self-willed powerhouse, laced with "grit and nails" of determination.

She has graced me with many letters over the years, but this letter was the cream of the crop. This letter, as all her letters are, was handwritten and ten pages long. I started the New Year off reading this letter, all of it, right after midnight. Every passionate, written page. It took about twenty minutes. Upon finishing this letter, I could not do anything but cry ... softly, tears of joy, sorrow, gratefulness, humbleness, and awe at the depth of this woman's soul, seasoned with years of knowledge about a culture that has been ripped apart.

Many of our people seem to feel no responsibility for repairing the hundreds of years of damage and defeat, making anything they attempt to do be a struggle of the mind and sometimes the body. She sees the world in its dimmest light as she peers through her own light-hued skin, which reminds her of our plight as people of color. She loves dark skin, as she appreciates the people she works so diligently for, a community of people who see her as a living billboard of buttons and slogans pertaining to police brutality. She wears the notes of a broken spirit. It is in her strength that I see our weaknesses.

How many of us could use our body as a human billboard every day, to keep our purpose in view, to bring about help for the mental illness that racism brews daily as we go about just trying to exist? I see her persistence as an opening to some of our issues. We "try," but we must begin to "do" and put *trying* away. Yes, after all the written definitions I have received from many people from different walks of life about a broken spirit—and I find we have all, in one way or another, experienced "broken spirit situations"—she hit the nail on the head. The trap that we find ourselves in is becoming deeper and deeper as we "think our way" farther down that "hole of destruction."

My heart goes out to my people, yet our garments of "flesh, bone, blood, and hair" are just that, garments. We are *spirits* having a human experience, so why are we having such a difficult time with the acceptance of our garments of color and especially darkened hues? Mother D. has been the watchman on the wall speaking against racism as an illness that needs attention like any illness. She will not give up and has chosen her own way to sacrifice her garment of flesh: to be that billboard.

I met an interesting gentleman that I and another person will be working together with, as planned, on radio. He gave a great analogy of how we can make a *shift* in this world's negative influences. He used the example of *cigarettes*. There was a time when people who did *not* smoke were standing on the outside of the restaurant looking into the window at the people who were eating and smoking inside, wishing for a smoke-free place to eat. Now today, nonsmokers sit and dine in total smoke-free environments, while smokers are on the outside looking in. Smoking once used to be *cool*, and now it carries a different adjective, as many don't understand why anyone would continue a destructive and unclean habit. *Thought* was transformed by putting awareness on something relentlessly.

As Mother D. says, along with so many other activists and people who know, *injustice to anyone is injustice for everyone.* She wants so desperately to see justice and fairness prevail.

Like the cigarette smokers, people who are "unjust practitioners " will have to be taught to *use* the mind that keeps them in the mindset of feeling superior *and* threatened, which is actually a type of fear of inferiority. Laws can be set to stop public smoking, but laws cannot control the mindset of how people think; that will take a new wave of positive thinking, the more we the people begin to think and use positive language, meditation, the very energy of the words and the thought processes will begin to flow like the microwaves, the electro-waves, and all the airborne technologies that we are bombarded with on a daily basis.

One day, sitting with Mother D. for about three hours in my studio apartment, one on one, I felt so honored to be able to have her to myself. As usual, she was with her sign and her buttons, as if her audience was the world. I was the first artist that she gave permission to paint her image. I met her long before she began her button garments and hat, about twenty-one years ago. I was searching for my culture and my history—I thought I had the spiritual thing in order.

Little did I know how much internal work I would do *through* the knowledge of our history and culture. The door to spiritual awareness was just beginning to really open up and show me how bits and pieces of my life were laced with this universal knowledge, and now I would be privy to a "pantry of spiritual nourishment." I had written children's stories based on these principles, started many of my community programs, such as Volunteer 2000, a program that explains how to get the whole community—commercial and private—to work together by the *universal laws of allowing, attraction, and gratitude.*

I am inspired by her dedication and drive, as she writes many letters to statesmen, council members, and lay members. Her fingers are priceless tools of the creative process no computer could achieve. I could feel her deep commitment to her purpose, but what touched me was her desire to honor and praise me for my work in the community of the art world, which I had entered at a late age. I moved quickly to the sort of top events that many artists wanted to be. I once had to explain to someone who said, "You have to pay your dues" that when God takes over a situation, one has no choice, and the dues a person pays is not to be judged by standards only God knows; these are paid in the heart of man.

Besides, I had paid my dues in many ways, and there would be more to come. My creativity was to make art as black as possible, to prove the positive attribute of blackness and how it was inclusive more than negative. I became as obsessed with using black paint as a Mother Dember is about her buttons. I was sometimes on public stages with renowned artists who insinuated that only *golden brown* skin was acceptable to use for skin tones, and I refused to back down on the beauty and the inclusiveness of *black*, stating, "You cannot accept any of us until you can accept the blackest of us." (AF)

I know there were times my black art locked me out. But other doors were opened to me by people who understood my passion and my message. Love seemed to be "blocked out" for my people, because of their dark skin. This low acceptance of black skin is not just a white issue, it is a black issue too, as we have so much self-hate. This is why it was more important for me to share this love for blackness, for the sake of Black people, more so than for non-blacks.

One day, a gallon of paint spilled out in my Honda Odyssey. Of course, what other color would it be … but black? Well, I always find a "reason" even for the "mistakes" in my life. Even when I spilled a gallon of white paint over black stones in my courtyard, it ended up being a very good spiritual lesson. I don't make a habit of spilling gallons of paint, but the black and the white were symbolic of my life mission.

This chapter is to reveal my purpose and plan to carry on Mothers Dember's pilgrimage. I have been working on the answer to this situation of racism. Love is the answer. We cannot make anyone love us, but we can love ourselves, and that is where we must start: by loving each other, loving ourselves. Once we master that, it will be so on point, because what you give, you get back. When love is given, it is like a "reflective armor plate." It will come back, because it is one of the laws of the universe: "what you give … will be given back."

I dedicate my mission to this woman of hard work, serious intentions, a dedicated wife, determined to be a mother and not be frightened off by many miscarriages, bringing five children into this world. She has supported me in the arts and in my decision to go back into the "trenches" of politics and organizations, to reach a people who we sometimes count as a lost. We are in a global world, an intercultural society, and we must be able to educate and inform *ourselves*.

These laws of the universe work for all God's creations; there is order in nature *and* disorder. Every situation has a positive and a negative side, for that is life. We have ridden the waves of slavery, torture, family destruction, male and female distrust, being taught to feel less than a man, treated less than animals. We are far better than just mere *men*, for we are spirit beings having a human experience in our garments of blood, bones, and various hues of skin, dark to light. We must begin to speak in positive dialogue with each other, to ourselves, with the intent to bring good to this whole world. And we are just the vessels to do it.

As long as we have strong people like Mother Dember. and the late Mama Delaney—her best friend and comrade, with a story of her own to be told, who transformed last year to go on to the ancestors and will not be forgotten—we can do it. I am just a drop in their footsteps, wanting to be a brighter light, shedding as much of this "human" without the "being" and be more of the *being*.

I bow in respect for a woman or man who is on her or his purpose. What is your purpose? Don't forget the story of the cigarettes—the ones on the inside at one time will be on the outside as time brings about a change of intent, defiance of purpose, and the breaking of the hypnotic rhythm (that which causes us to do the same thing over and over).

The only hypnotic rhythm I want is one of love and devotion to bringing justice and human rights to all people, and restoring the dignity, the joy, and the culture of a people who have long been invisible at the table of life.

So I have spotlighted *The Three Sisters* in this chapter, because these three women have crossed my life and many others with inspiration. I am giving them honor in this book, for I know them personally, and they have experienced many broken spirits over their lives. Each would be in the category of Elder. Many of us look up to them as Mother figures. The last of these is ...

Akua looking forward
By Akua

Inspiration

I Did Not Build "My Life" by Myself

My desire to fulfill the purpose of sharing the ways to healing a broken spirit comes through my life lessons and my personal experiences, which were sometimes not the best moments that I am proud of. But from an early age, God has guided me and kept me from many things that I have witnessed in my own family, my relationships, my community, and in my church. He has kept me out of the depths of a place called the Bloody Fifth, a name that was true to the depths, as many people lost loved ones. I too lost three to the streets of the Fifth Ward and one to the Third Ward. Yet by the grace of God and a mother who raised us with dignity, even though we did not always have our lights, gas, or water on, we were taught to be clean, respectful, and to hold our heads up high. My tall sisters were taught not to slump but to walk erect. Even though I was average (and to some "short"—though I never owned that!), I walked as if I had the height of a six-foot model. My love for my mother overrode any imperfection that she had—and she had a few that caused me some irritation. Her love and devotion also overwhelmed any imperfections—even the one that changed the meaning of my existence as to who I thought I was (but God had other plans for my DNA to be different; I used to wonder why I felt so different from all of my siblings).

As the youngest, I felt a loneliness that I learned to fill with a creative mind in poetry, design, and thoughts of life and its purpose. I was also always visiting and talking to people, building relationships along the way throughout my life—there are many people I have met along the way, some just for a reason and some for a season.

I wanted the definition of *broken spirit* to come from different places, different levels of education and social status. I believe everyone is *regular people*; some just have been able to move to different levels on the "stairway of life," of human opportunity.

Due to the beautiful responses I got from the participants of this chapter, I knew right away part II of *Broken Spirits* would be called *Making the Connection to Wholeness.*

I believe the majority of organizations and many business ventures derive from some form of broken spirit, either of the person who creates it or from the experiences of being with others who needed healing. This book will include one of the earliest promises that I made to a dear friend whose whole family is dedicated to love and service to the community. These folks have no organization or business, but they serve so many in the community with their giving and sharing hearts. The father, Ernest Goodrich, experienced a life-threatening illness but is on the mend and still serving, sometimes to a fault. He understands that everyone has value as humans, and his story will be an example of those to be shared in the coming book. *Mrs.* Goodrich is the type of woman who has been a godsend to her family in many ways, and to me.

I apologize for those who sent me material that did not make it into this book, but I assure you, it will be considered for the second edition, as I feel it will better serve the purpose of that one. This book is based on my personal story, which I was told to write and share as the many broken situations I had to survive and thrive from. But I wanted to share a part of it with those who have crossed my path in one way or another.

I want to send out a special thanks for those who participated, some who I was so surprised to hear from, that gave beautiful statements, and some who I expected to participate but did not. I am happy with the outcome, so maybe it was not a good idea for those to participate this time around. The beauty of a healing spirit is to be confident in what you are being led to do, even if some think you are not ripe for the challenge. It was you who pushed me harder, by not participating. It made me press even harder to finish on time. Thanks to all of you who are in the book and to you who are not.

Broken Spirits as Defined from the Community

The first recorded definition of a broken spirit goes back before the creation of mankind. According to Biblical history, the earth was a place where the first broken spirits were sent. This is in reference to God casting Lucifer and the fallen angels down to earth. A broken spirit is the disconnection between the mental, the spiritual, and the physical connection to God. For example, insanity is a form of a broken spirit. However, when we are in our mother's womb, we are blessed with a fully connecting spirit. Therefore, because of Lucifer, we are born into a world filled with broken spirits. In this world of suffering, a broken spirit can be obtained through tragedy. This is my definition from a personal experience of my mother dying in my arms.

—Imhotep

My greatest fear is that I may speak the wrong thing. I do not like to speak untruths; in my life, my spirit has been broken. I am always reading, thinking, and listening for the word of God, dedicating my life to God … But, Satan knows my weakness … I depend on God who knows more about me, as I wait not knowing when the time will come. My fear *is my brokenness … That I work on.*

—Isaac

A broken spirit is a diagnosis for having an anti-spiritual disease that eats on your spirit as you live thru some irreversible, forever life-changing event that has no explanation, for example an unexpected death. However, time is an antibiotic for the spirit, a priceless gift from the universe. It can heal what we cannot see and how we feel.

—Chrystal
In memory of my EEB

A broken spirit to me is when you have allowed the devil to jeopardize your relationship with God to the affect that you have lost respect for you and God.

—Ollie H.

I remember writing a story in school, and my teacher humiliated me by saying she knew I would be writing the next chapter for the following assignment, implying that I had plagiarized my story. It stopped me from writing for years.

—Edgar

My broken spirit is when I first realized that I was a sinner before God and that Jesus was beaten unmercifully for me, for the healing of my body, and died for all of the sins I've done. I'm amazed at the wonderment.

Thank you, Jesus, for your love.

—Sarah

My definition of "broken spirit" is sorrow.

My heart has been painfully crushed and my spirit and soul are out of order. I am crippled by my inner pain. My family traditions and togetherness have been shattered, so I lean on God as my crutch. I let go, let God, and now I have the courage and strength to continue my journey, without sorrow.

—June E

A broken spirit is a hole in the soul.

Self seeps out daily, with nobody to staunch the bleeding but you.

Its gaping hole shows all your pain, obscene in its nakedness.

An agony so intense, you embrace death, forgetting spirit is eternal, and only God sutures ravaged souls.

—Trinidad

Broken Spirits (That Broke Other Spirits)

When I received the call from Sista' Akua to contribute to this project called Broken Spirits, *I was happy and humbled at the same time. In less than a nanosecond, the broken spirit of my inner child blasted out of me. Just like so many times in my almost 59 years on earth, whenever conversations of such sensitive topics are discussed, my inner child clamors to be* heard, *not just listened to, but really heard, hopefully understood, and finally, just maybe have my issues resolved. However, the more I reflected on this subject matter, I eventually came face to face with my very own painful, honest truth.*

To be completely open with you and before I continue, I must acknowledge that not only have I been married since 09/29/79 and that I'm the proud father of two grown children, but on 12/17/90, I was admitted into a rehabilitation facility for my "crack" addiction. Those of you who currently or in the past loved, lived with, endured, or otherwise witnessed the self-destruction of a "crack-head" can appreciate the fact that while my family celebrates my 22 years of sobriety this year, it in no way erases the heartache and pain they suffered during my addiction. Therefore, in final analysis, not only am I a victim, but I'm also a perpetrator of "broken spirits." Now, that's an extremely painful fact of my life that I swore I'd NEVER *subject my children to, yet I'm guilty as charged.*

The source of my broken spirits, my anger, and my pain was my hero, my god, and the one person I modeled myself after. Of course, I'm referring to my father. I clearly recall the happy days before that *painful night. I remember riding with him as he made deliveries of fresh-baked bread, and being able to eat it straight from the oven. I remember him carrying my oldest brother home on his shoulders after my brother hit a little league inside-the-park game-winning homerun, and just knowing that one day I'd enjoy the very same experience. Most of all, I remember him taking us over to his brother's house (that I was named in honor of), and my two older brothers and I performing for the neighbors that Uncle E. had gathered to see us. Yes, those were my "good old days." Since we lived in the Chicago projects, it wasn't too depressing when my parents separated and eventually divorced, because we still spent time with him.*

But then came "that" night.

When I was about 13 years old, my dad came to visit one night, and I remember him paying me back the $5 that he'd borrowed from me. I thought it was like any other visit. Little did I know that I wouldn't see him again for about 10 years. Later, I found out that he took his savings and left town that very night, without even saying good-bye. Didn't he know I needed him, that he was my hero, my god, my role model? Didn't he care? Needless to say, I was CRUSHED. *My heart crumbled, my spirits smashed, my self-esteem and self-confidence teetering on the edge of oblivion and pushed over that edge, when time after time and year after year being told lie after lie by him. My only alternative was to* HATE *my dad,* HATE *my God and finally* HATE *myself.*

At the time, I didn't realize I had turned to drugs for relief, I just started smoking marijuana and drinking because it felt good. Over time, using drugs became a daily occurrence No Matter What, *and by the time I graduated to "crack," any day that ended with a* y *was an excuse to sneak off, lie about something, start an argument about nothing, or even steal money from my wife's purse. My behavior during my addiction most assuredly broke the spirits of my angel of a wife and my innocent children, just as horrendously as my dad broke mine.*

However, we have persevered, I have a new, better relationship with my very own higher power, that I identify as Mother-Father God, and that works for me. Every day I try to continue to make amends to my family for the wreckage of my past, to be a better person, and to set a good example for my children, family, and friends. My family has forgiven me as I have forgiven Dad, and although we still go through our daily-living issues, we are living proof that even "broken spirits" can heal and become "whole spirits" once again.

—Earnest B.

Top view of painting

Dec 16, 2012 1:18 a.m.

No Joy or Peace,
My spirit cries.
Fill my heart.
My spirit cries.
When I feel shattered, broken, or despised …
My broken heart cries.

No Hope or Dreams,
My spirit cries.
Fill my mind,
My spirit cries.
When I feel shattered, broken or compromised …
My broken heart cries.

So I saw no promise of the days gone by,
For my broken spirit was shattered, broken, and unsatisfied …
So through those shed tears
My broken spirit cries … to be mended, tended, and redefined …

—Dee

A Broken Spirit and a Remedy

Often we read the Scriptures about a broken spirit. A broken spirit and a broken heart seem to be synonymous. As a pastor, I witness many occasions where I have seen members experiencing what I determined to be broken in spirit.

Death can cause a broken spirit when it is a loved one's relationship that has been severed. Loss of employment, personal or financial setbacks, all of these can cause a broken spirit. What I do know is that God does not cause *your broken spirit. He seeks to heal it with joy and happiness.*

Proverbs 15:13 says, "A merry heart maketh a cheerful countenance, but by sorrow of the heart, the Spirit is broken." Jesus Christ experienced a crushed, but not a broken spirit in the Garden of Gethsemane when he said to the father, "If it be possible, let this cup pass, but not my will, but thy will be done." The psalmist also helps those that experience broken spirit or heart by letting us know what God will do. Psalm 147:3 tells us "[God] healeth the broken in heart and bindeth up their wounds." When my *spirit feels crushed, I rely on the words of Jesus in John 14:1:"Let not your heart be troubled: ye believe in God, believe also in me."*

As a pastor, I believe every word Jesus says, because he is a master at repairing brokenness.

—Pastor James E. N

Man has a spirit. He is a flesh and blood mortal.

Man's spirit inhabits his brain, distinguishing it from the animal brain. Some animals have a larger brain than man's brain, but they have animal instincts. The spirit in man's brain gives him the superiority to rule the animal kingdom.

Man's spirit can be broken. What I mean is trauma or tragedy can break man's spirit. Like losing a close loved one or seeing a loved one suffer through death or an illness that cannot be healed. Some men have committed suicide over such things as losing one's financial ability. A broken spirit arises or man can turn to the Creator or to the Evil One when he is broken. Some few turn to the Evil One to get even. Some to God, who uses a broken spirit to do good for mankind.

Man's spirit is the intelligence that keeps this age going. Airplanes, computers, the medical professions, city building—this is all the creation of the spirit in man.

—Milton R.

Our inner spirit gives us hope. When one's spirit is broken, there is no hope because there has been a disconnect between that which gives us hope (our inner guide to our Source) and our mind.

—Akelay

The following are my thoughts on "broken spirit":

A "broken spirit" is a desperate sadness, a deep aloneness, a feeling of being stuck in pain with few choices on how it can be relieved. There is a deep disconnect from a sense of self or purpose in life; and little faith in connecting with a beneficent power greater than oneself.

Each of these "broken spirit" challenges in my life helped me to learn how to reach out to friends and or family. As a result, I found the treasures of joy, serenity, and gratitude.

I have less fear today. I know now to garden and connect with mother nature, call a friend or family member and connect with human nature, or to meditate and be still and connect with my "quiet nature." I trust that the universe takes care of itself, and if I get out of the way, the right people come into my life right when I need them.

My spirit does not break as deeply anymore, even though difficulties still occur. I can feel them now and know what to do if my spirit begins to "crack" again. I know this difficult time is a time for growth; joy is possible again. In knowing my pain, I also, experience my joys much more richly.

I have a quiet knowing that every life experience brings me closer to a fuller sense of my best self.

—Anonymous

When a spirit is truly broken, it gives in to hopelessness, completely. It turns nowhere, for it looks nowhere and in no direction. The true, broken spirit may occupy a physical body (a human shell), but it feels nothing. It is ... a hallow being with no punishment.

—L. Hawkins

Betty, the oldest girl living, out of the six born, has been through things like all of us. She left home early and was the first to marry and bring grandchildren to our lives. One place of brokenness that she can relate to is that of her loss of memory after the loss of her husband, Paul, of fifty years plus. The frustration and the disconnect of the loss of losing a loved one can cause a disconnect that makes it difficult to move forward; fear and loneliness can be its companion. But with the constant memory of the love of God, this too can be overcome, and we are all wanting her to return to living her best life.

As we all are in our years of reaping our harvest, we must still be mindful of the harvest that we have created and share our love and forgiveness with one another.

This is written by Akua at the request of
—B.J Davis

Broken spirit—there is no connection with God. Feeling depressed, unhappy, hopeless,unworthy, and disheartened.

Thanks!

—Keshia

What a Broken Spirit Means to Me

When I began to wake up from my sickness, although I appeared to be whole, I would find that some things were broken. I have to categorize them.

The first one I discovered was the spirit of oneness. Whereas my mind, which had never disobeyed my brain, was broken, and later my spirit would try to follow it, I would not allow that. Instead, I chose to fight to save my spirit. The spirit of humility. I felt as if I was on display, where the whole world could see my nakedness, and I no longer had privacy. Different nurses and family members would see parts of my body, which normally would be hidden by clothing, regardless of how I felt about it. The spirit of identity, I could not recognize myself. l became a complete stranger to myself. Without my memories and loving family, I could have easily forever lost myself. Even today, I don't give up on finding me. I see glimpses of me but never feel the totality of Clifford Darnell Francis.

I guess I can't honestly answer this question, because my spirit has never been broken, and I intend to never experience it. It is my sincere belief that the God I serve will never allow it. He is my spirit, and He cannot be broken. I hope this helps.

—Clifford

Broken Spirit

No faith no future.
Lose your belief and your inspiration is gone,
Dreams dissipated …

—Dwight T.

The Death of Me

Call out the mourners, make deep the grave
For a girl named Cherry has just passed away.
Summon the preacher to do his part with words of how
she died of a broken heart.
Not too many pallbearers, for her body is light.
Her flesh seemed to leave her night after night.

I remember her well and how she would dance with joy
and took on everyone's troubles, be it girl or boy.
Oh how she lived with the greatest of ease, never caring
what others may say; she did as she pleased.

Life was her carnival; she rode all the rides.
Even on stormy seas, she mastered the tide.
People were her thing, she would always say,
and she loved them and cared for them in a very gentle way.

But something happened to our Cherry so gay,
somehow her spirit just slipped away.

Don't send flowers, for they are for the living.
Remember the people around you, and to them do the
giving.

I knew her quite well and all she wanted to be.
Of course I knew her well, for that girl is me.

—Cherry S.

Broken Spirit

Broken Spirit is a brutal coming of age. Broken Spirit comes from learning that what you believed about your world and your place in it is not true. You must become someone else, moving with blind faith into that becoming.

Best wishes,

—Alexis Brooks

To me a spirit is faith/hope not only in God but also in tomorrow and life in general. For one to have a broken spirit is to lose hope in living and to keep pushing in through the storm. Basically, a broken spirit is the lack of hope for a better tomorrow.

—Isaiah H

What a Broken Spirit Means to Me

A broken spirit is a broken path, split with a fork in the road. It is a place where crucial decision-making takes place. Where to turn? When I walked on the broken road paved with the spirit of pride, lies, or sadness, I was burdened with the choice: stay or leave. I chose to leave … or at least I tried. When I turned to myself, the spirit of pride blinded me from seeing others. When I turned to the world (everybody else), the spirit of lies blinded me from seeing truth. When I turned my attention to my wounds, the spirit of sadness blinded me from seeing beauty.

I quickly (and sometimes not so quickly) learned that I turned the wrong corner, but I still kept searching for a way out. I ultimately turned a different corner and ran smack into a Brick Wall. I was in pain, but upon that Wall was written the Promises of God. Crushed by the hard truth and broken by the spirit of pride, lies, and sadness, I finally sat still and listened to God's voice and respected His authority. He whispered to me James 4:6 (God resists the proud but gives grace to the humble;); *Proverbs 19:9* (……….. and a liar will be destroyed.).

I heard His warning. In return, He heard my cry, granted me His mercy, and healed me with Hebrews 12:11 (For the moment, all discipline seems painful rather than pleasant, but later it yields the peaceful fruit of righteousness to those who have been trained by it.). *Through 2 Corinthians 12:9 (*My grace is sufficient for you, for my power is made perfect in weakness.*), He told me to get up and follow Him.*

I still find myself on the wrong road sometimes. But by the grace of God, I always know how to return to the path that is good and true. In Psalm 119:105 (Your word is a lamp to my feet and a light to my path.*), I find peace in knowing that when I get hurt and broken by others or my own beliefs, God takes joy in that moment of my brokenness, because I am ripe to be rescued by His wisdom, hope, and mercy. I always have a place to find refuge; Psalm 34: 17–20* (When the righteous cry for help, the Lord hears and delivers them out of all their troubles. The Lord is near to the brokenhearted and saves the crushed in spirit. Many are the afflictions of the righteous, but the Lord delivers him out of them all.).

I am thankful for a broken spirit, because it ultimately has led me to personally experience God and develop a love for Him and His ways. There is no greater gift than to be taught to love God. For those who love God, a broken spirit is a hard place with a soft landing: Romans 8:28 (And we know that for those who love God all things work together for good, for those who are called according to his purpose.).

—Lisa

A broken spirit is when you are truly defeated. It is that feeling of giving up. It was like what I went through when I lost my mother—nothing was important to me anymore, not my husband, my children, and not even myself.

Actually I was lost in my sorrow.

The struggle is over; the situation is resolved when you can see who is in control: God.

A broken spirit does not represent a broken or destroyed life. *Only that you're lost in the sorrow and pain of what you are going through, like when you lose someone that was a major part of you. For me, my mother.*

—Yvonne R.

I weep, I cry.
My countenance is low.
I sleep, I die.
My heart bleeds the well dry.
I weep the tears of a broken spirit.
And early in the morning I awaken with a sad heart and tear-stained sheets.
But I awake anew, like a weary traveler that stumbles on a refreshing brook.
I awake with a prayer. Yes, sweet prayer and many prayers on my lips, as prayer is the answer.
I pray for peace. Yes peace! His peace! That kind of peace, that surpasses all human understanding.
He gives me peace!
I pray for comfort. Comfort is desperately needed. The comfort of an unborn baby in her mother's womb or in the safety of a father's strong arms after his boy recovers from a bad dream.
He comforts me!
I pray for joy. Why Joy? Because it's been told by those of old that "pain may endure for a night, but joy comes in the morning."
I am happy!
I pray for restoration, because only He can restore my broken and distraught spirit. It needs to be mended, refreshed, renewed, recharged, and restored. He does that for me.
I smile, I live.

—Charles

Healing and Hope

I was around nine years old at the time. My mother & father had a horrible marriage, and & sadly, I was their audience. The details are beyond anything one could imagine. Okay … 4th grade & nine years old, I was a depressed, little, insecure kid. My mom & dad separated, & I chose to live with my dad. Either choice was "gonna be hell". Would I stay with my mother, who was having an extramarital affair with an abusive man (to her), or would I choose to go with my emotionally abusive father? Either way, I was destined for emptiness & despair. At that time, my life was a living hell.

I will also call this "Broken Spirit/Angels/& Ray of Hope" ... God blessed me bigtime.

On a regular school day, I would sometimes cry & not realize that I was bringing attention to myself. One day, my father came to pick me up from school & at the end of the day proceeded to cause a major scene by spanking me in front of the entire school for "acting up." It gave the other kids a story to gossip with each other about & take home to Mom & Dad. By that time, I was in the spotlight & not in a happy way. So not only was I depressed at home, but I feared going to school. There was no happy/safe/ secure place for me to be. Many teachers understood & knew my situation, yet there was nothing they could do to rescue me.

Here we go with "Broken Spirit" ... "Healing & Hope" ...

At my elementary school, there was a lady who managed the cafeteria named Valarie. This lady radiated love & kindness to every child who passed through that line daily. After all these years, just telling this story brings tears of joy to my eyes.

Somehow, one afternoon, as she was wrapping up her day, I stopped by to see her & say hi. (To this day, I have no clue if Valarie knew my hopeless situation.) She took time to stop & visit with me. The following may not sound like much ... yet ... she said something like ... "Johnny, we have some of your favorite cake left over ... would you like to take some home with you?"

The sections of cake were a wonderful act of kindness, although those slices of cake were like simple acts of love *to me. She probably had no idea the hope that she brought me. Slices of gold! Over the school year, I would visit with her on many afternoons. For her to take a break & talk to me was a lifeline. Regardless, she took the time. What an Angel she was!*

That would have been around 1961/62. In 1988, when I was on Houston radio, I again was telling my childhood story & located Valarie, who was elderly & retired. I picked up the phone and called her to remind her how much she meant to me so many years ago, for a lost little boy. Letting her know how she simply gave me her time & slices of cake to take home & to believe in a brighter tomorrow. I'm so happy that I never let her forget the love & hope for a brighter day.

I'm a blessed person indeed. Hopefully my short story will give someone the desire to look back at those who made a difference in YOUR *life and pass on that Ray of Hope.*

—Johnny G

As I began to put the chapters of this book in place and checked to see if all was ready to go to the editor, I smiled as my Spirit told me it was now the time to look up the *dictionary* definitions of *broken* and *spirit*. Some would say that should have been my first research before writing the book, but I felt, just as in my art, I wanted my own definition to be raw and from me, inspired by my life experience and, of course, my knowledge of what broken is and what spirit seems to be. But for those who like the official definitions that the dictionary gives, I would so agree that a *spirit* can be "broken," as in the example of what brokenness does to anything broken.

Webster's New Universal Unabridged Dictionary

I love old dictionaries, and this has a 1972 copyright.

Broken:

Broken*:* parted by violence into two or more pieces or fragments; splintered; fractured.
Interrupted … as in *broken sleep.*
Violated, unfulfilled … as in *broken laws, broken promises.*
Not fluent, imperfectly spoken … as in *broken speech.*
Crushed, humbled … as a *broken spirit.*

Weakened: enfeebled; made infirmed *as in broken health, broken constitution* [a word I heard my mother use concerning her ill health … but while stating her constitution was strong!].

Subdued, tamed, trained … as a *broken colt.*

Ruined in resources … as in *bankruptcy*

In painting, reduced in tone by adding mixture of gray; said of a color … as *broken color.*

Broken-backed: having a broken back, worn-out, shattered.

Broken down: worn out, shattered, disheartened, broken in health or spirit.

Brokenhearted: having the spirits depressed or crushed by grief or despair.

SPIRIT

Spirit: the soul life, from the Latin *spirare,* to blow, to breathe.

> (a) the life principle, especially in man, originally regarded as an animating vapor infused by breath;
> (b) or as bestowed by a Deity, the soul;
> (c) the thinking, motivating part of man, distinguished from the body: mind, intelligence, thought, etc. … regarded as separate from matter;
> (d) a supernatural being of a certain good or evil character, etc.; angel or demon, fairy or elf.

Often the frame of the mind, disposition, mood, temper … as in *good spirits.*

Real meaning, true intentions … as in *spirit of the law.*

Due to a certain condition of the mind, a broken spirit can make someone feel better or worse in life. Someone should try and figure out the cause and effect of a situation before trying to solve a problem. In spite of all the struggles and repercussions, good or bad, one goes through, he or she can share thoughts with God and some positive people and try to move on in a joyful way.

Survival is one of the keys to a broken spirit. Grace will help too. Grace is amazing.

—Olevia R.

To me a spirit is faith/hope not only in GOD but also in tomorrow and life in general, for one to have a broken spirit is to lose hope in living and to keep pushing in through the storm. Basically a broken spirit is the lack of hope for a better tomorrow

— Ishmael /Baby

What a Broken Spirit Means to Me

While working for Texas' prison system right out of high school, I witnessed the faces of some broken spirits. Some of these people had no more hopes, no more dreams or aspirations. Something within them stopped living because of the pain that they felt and the situation they felt they were in. To live with a broke spirit means to lose interest in seeking joy. Once a person's spirit is broken, they don't see the sun shine or feel the warmth of the sun on a cool day—they don't see the rainbow in the sky because they're still concentrating on the rain that has already subsided.

My spirit has been broken before, like theirs. But after my spirit has been healed over and over, it takes more distraught to break it again. I guess broken spirits make you stronger.

—D. Douglas

A broken spirit is when people live ungodly lives;
When a person has a broken and contrite heart

Unnamed.

What pleases God more than sacrifices is a humble heart that looks to him when trouble crushes and one pleads for mercy when sin has been committed.

—Jimmie

What is a Broken Spirit? Where do it comes from; and can it be healed?

I think A Broken Spirit, is the inability to feel whole and complete; for many people, this disconnect began a few months after birth; and it is totally man made. Doing the nine months when the mother carries her baby; she tries to do everything within her powers, to make sure she has a healthy child. Somewhere between the 4th and the 5th month of pregnancy; the mother establishes a close relationship with her baby. She may sing to her unborn child as she goes about her daily chores... or... she may just speak softly to the baby... while compassionately rubbing her stomach. This loving and bonding relationship continues right through birth

—Jo. Burrell

Note from the author:

The rest of this theory on babies and broken spirit will appear in the part II of Healing a Broken Spirit, where it will be discussed from birth to old age how our spirits are broken and in need of repair.

A broken spirit isn't something that can be easily defined on a sheet of paper; nor can it wear a label and apply to everyone. It is like clouds above our heads—none are the same yet none are different. It covers over every being, every heart we know. Some are tangible, some invisible.

Some are noticeable, others cower in the darkness. Everyone has one, and everyone knows one. To find your broken spirit, first find your heart.

—Nia

A broken spirit to me is a spirit that is disconnected to its higher self or higher purpose. The disconnection from one's higher (God's) spirit is self-explanatory. Higher purpose is different. So many are broken because they are not in tune to why they are here and fulfilling their spirits true purpose that God made just for them.

—D. Evans

What a Broken Spirit Means to Me

When you lose hope, when faith is destroyed, when willpower ceases the desire to go on, you have embraced some of the ills of a broken spirit.

At the core of our inner most being lays our spirit. At times, the spirit even reflects the essence of who we really are; it represents us when we are on the many stages of life. Our spirit is so interwoven into our lives that you can almost wear it. But when the spirit is broken our innermost self becomes affected.

When I think about a broken spirit I am reminded of a time in my life when rejection and a feeling of self- worth and belonging crushed my spirit – leaving me engulfed with sadness dramatically. For many years I lived with a broken spirit. Although on the surface one could hardly tell, as a result of my suppressing it, I nevertheless suffered inwardly without understanding how to fix it.

At its worst, a broken spirit carries various dysfunctions, i.e., a loss of simple enjoyment, mental and emotional depression, thoughts of suicide, and even the act of suicide. When we come against circumstances that overtake us, depending on our mental capacity and emotional strength will depend on how we handle the broken spirit. For me it took reliving those ugly moments analytically to fully understand exactly what occurred that triggered my spirit causing it to become broken.

Finally I had to come to realization that the understanding of oneself is the single most important part of the restoring of a broken spirit. Only then could my hope, will, faith, and ultimately broken spirit be healed.

—C. R. Francis

What is a broken spirit? Mine was a broken spirit. Evil was ever-present, blocking anything good around me. Evil breaks spirits by assaulting our faith in God like Satan did to Jesus in the wilderness.

Blindsided, emotionally lobotomized, and blinded, I was broken. Jesus healed me. I'm no longer a broken spirit.

—M. Harris

A broken spirit is a temporary state when the enemy wants us to feel hopeless. Yet God gives us a word … "I can do all things through Christ who strengthens me" (Phil. 4:13). And I am renewed.

—Dr. P. Atkins

Suffering from a broken spirit I know all too well. A broken spirit is the spirit of brokenness, which leaves you feeling helpless, depressed—feeling down and out! The reason why I say this is I've made poor choices in the areas of relationships, career, and money issues.

Somehow when making choices you're not thinking whether there are consequences attached to that choice. And that was me! The repercussions were just that severe. I made the choice to walk away from a good paying job that I hated to its core. In my mind, I could find a job in a New York minute. However, that minute turned into days, weeks … nearly a year. I felt down and out. More than anything, I felt depressed and completely broken.

In the midst of my brokenness, I prayed! I prayed earnestly for understanding/knowledge, prayed for answers, for solutions, and for deliverance! The more I prayed, the deeper my depression got. Still, in the midst of my brokenness, I never ceased praying or believing for deliverance! And as a result of praying and keeping the faith, the spirit from within touched me in a loving way whereas I was able to pray for forgiveness!

This was powerful. I did just that—prayed for forgiveness. In the midst of praying for forgiveness I was able to understand how to make better choices. From that moment, I learned to forgive myself. Later, that broken spirit was overcome by the spirit of forgiveness! I was no longer broken. I was free!

—Cassandra F.

I think a broken spirit is when you believe in God, then something happens in your life that strays you away from the Holy Spirit.

—Evelyn H.

A broken spirit is one who has yet to surrender all of the self. There is a spirit of God that is in every soul waiting to be set free.

—P. Wilder

Whenever one feels helpless, living for oneself, not pursuing to help others along the way—to make things better and peaceful. When each person learns it is not all about what you can do for you … but what you can do for others.

—Dr. Edith. I. Jones

A broken spirit to me is losing faith within yourself. Letting everything you've been through and still going through tear you down, in every situation you face in your everyday life. A broken spirit is walking around like nothing is wrong, putting others before yourself because you want their acceptance and friendship. Trying to find that purpose you once had in life, that is now not so clear/familiar to you.

Fearing in walking outside because you don't know if harm will be done to you when you once could walk at any time freely and carefree. That broken spirit is my mom, my dad—that broken spirit is you! But most of all that broken spirit is me!

—A young lady, about twenty-one

> Here me, for I am not your vessel .I have not fallen into despair
> nor darkness.
> Though my waters trimmer from not fear, but uncertainty.
> Broken spirit can you not see in my time of need, of reassurance is not an
> Invitation, for I am not your vessel.
> Broken spirit you are the fears and despair of man.
> You break spiritual connections from our temple which un-allows
> us to talk with our higher power or feel its blessings.
> Broken Spirit you tend to bring false warmth to backs…
> Often found on walls!
> When you are a "broken Spirit" the want and desire for love, attention,
> success, and fulfillment of filling the trench in which makes you
> a broken spirit.
> "I have not lost my will to fight and I have not lost my connection
> to my temple… though my "waters trimmer"
> I will not become a broken Spirit for You Are not "My Vessel "!!!
>
> —Bud….

My life has its roots in overlapping stages of despair and futility, often reflective in being crushed and defeated. While feeling paralyzed and locked into this indefiniteness of purpose for more years than I care to admit, at times it also became a comfort zone for that all too familiar state of bondage. Having successfully navigated the shores of discernment, when I can, literally, count it all JOY' in the midst of a storm, love my enemy, forgive myself and others, pray for those who spitefully use me. Faith and determination allows me to then press on through hardships, insults, disappointment, chaos, and persecutions {His grace is sufficient for me and His power is made perfect in weakness}. I further realize the trials and tests were for a far greater purpose, so I can confidently boast of my weaknesses, recognizing the inherent growth potential.

—B. Gregory

Broken Spirit

The pathway of life can surely create confusion, challenge our truth, cause concerns, foster doubt, and even fear. Those faithful to the true purpose, having a strong connection with the spirit may be perceived as "broken" and feel broken when actually it the spirit is only diverted, creating a temporary condition of the fleshly aspect being human.

Those truly connected to their creator are never of broken spirit we tarry to testify life's way that the spirit is divine.

—M. Barnes

A broken spirit that feels alone, disappointed, without hope, betrayed, abandoned. Lost, confused and disconnected from any sense of normalcy. I asked a friend whose husband had died suddenly in a car accident what is a broken spirit? She answered me. ", Be kinder than necessary, for everyone you meet is fighting some kind of battle."

—Alberta W.C

What is a Broken Spirit?
A spirit that suffered devastation
Whether from need or want.

The loss feels just as great!
The beauty in a broken spirit
Is the possibility of healing.

—T. Melonco

Broken spirits are far too prevalent in our society today, the unwillingness to put your children and yourself first is the alarming evidence that there is an overabundance of lack of self.

—S. Sterling

My mama always wanted a house...As a young woman I worked and saved until one day I was able to make that possible...not having a home was one of the things that I felt caused my mother to have a broken spirit .

—Sis Obama

To lose someone or to be abandoned by someone you care about ... like losing a person by death or someone who abandoned you as a kid.

—Written by a nine-year-old boy without editing ... Israel

Note from the author: I place this statement by a young man who is nine—I say young man because he is brilliant when it comes to the intellect of life. He once did a YouTube video, "Why I want the First Black President of the United States" ... I saved his for last because if a child understands his spirit can be broken ... Then we have work to do on the causes and the effects. Of course it is the effects that we have more control over due to the fact that there will always be in this physical world of unexpected events and problems, that we can only do our own work and duty to be better and have less broken spirits ...

The Spirit of Sister Friendship

I found a wonderful lifetime friend at a resale shop. We have been friends now, over twenty-three years. We have seen what living can do, and we appreciate having someone you can call who can feel your energy, be it high or low, and end up being that "ingredient" that can help you prevent a broken-spirit moment.

Glenda wrote a letter for HBSI to tell me of what she found in me as a friend.

Friends are priceless, and I am blessed to have more than a handful of good friends.

☕ ☕ ☕

At Martha's Vineyard Resale Shop, I found you, a treasure of a friend. We clicked—that's all I can say. Your warm smile and bright eyes, strong spirit, and willingness to share and listen drew me to you. I had found a sister!

As a newly single parent I was struggling to raise four young children between the age of three and twelve. I welcomed your good advice and your willingness to let me vent my issues. And I still do. You always encourage me no matter what I am going through. I have always felt loved, valued, and blessed.

I am nurtured and refreshed in the sanctuaries that you create. These spaces have offered me the peace and energy that I have needed to renew my energy at several points in my life. Sharing a meal, a cup of coffee, checking out the bookstore is great with you because you are so much fun to be with.

I want you to know that I am one of your greatest fans. I am a fan of the friendship and marriage that you and Ishman have. Thank you for being a good wife. Even though I am single now, it blesses me to be around you. I love the way you always put him first in your life. How awesome it is to watch your family grow up and be the community we have talked and you have worked to build for so long.

I appreciate your energy and willingness to right wrongs. You listen carefully to what people say to you, and you believe them when they show you. Your experiences in the community have shown me what can happen when people care. Your voice is beautiful, and I enjoy the words, stories, and dreams that come out of you. I always have. I am so glad that God allowed you to be in the media because you work for him.

Now the thing that I am so excited about: that the community hears you. We are touched and motivated by your love for us. This is what we always talked about, and here we are, a part of a vibrant and energetic community that is living Kwanzaa. It looks like God has partnered us for this journey, and I am looking forward to it.

You have never pushed your beliefs on me, and I have always embraced most them. But seriously—I see Jesus in you, doing God's business everywhere you go. There are some things that I would like to see changed. One is to let me help you more. It will bless me and help me to develop. We could support each other in organizing our space. I think we would probably be a great help to each other in this area. And last but not least, I want to see your house!

Angel flowing painting by Akua
On Kanara by Jimbo

My Personal Observations

I knew before I finished writing this book that a second edition was coming. While writing this book, my life did leaps, jumps, dips, flips, and a few rolls. I soon learned it was to help me on my journey and give me the spiritual muscles that I needed to face the things I still had to face.

The loss of loved ones through death is understandable, but loss due to being totally shut out is what I call a "death by default." That is when one chooses to X you out of their life with no conversation or argument that has led you to that condition. In other words, you are left wondering why.

I go back to some words of warning given by the Buddhist monk, along with the affirmation that I was a loving support to this person and for me not to worry, they would be all right. It was funny, because at the time there were no signs that I could see this coming, but it did.

I have truly been in the "valley" and trust me, it is a lifesaver, a mind defender, and a way of peace when there is none.

So many great blessings have come my way in the process of writing this book, but not without the pains of life, which sometimes can be used as rocket fuel or stepping stones. It all depends on how well I am grounded on the *road to my destiny*. I use the automobile as a metaphor for *me* and the road for the *path* to my purpose. I have been on the gravel a number of times, and a few times in the dirt, but thanks to the use of prayer, meditation, the acknowledgment of spiritual guides at my side for the asking, I have avoided the embankment or the ditch.

In other words, managing and observing my thoughts, appreciating where I am and who I am, in the present moment, from day to day, I can more than survive this journey. I can thrive and help others as others are helping me.

Some of the lessons I have learned are profound in helping us to learn that there is no strict process to raising a perfect—or even acceptable—child. As long as we are given the ability to *choo*se, the possibility of going left or going right exists in the lives of individuals. I am learning to be less judgmental … and learning how to be a better judge. The difference is that one condemns the person and the other considers how to correct—or eradicate—*behavior.*

To condemn someone based on *my* perception is not healthy, for it puts me in the way of being condemned. To *judge* is to place myself or my loved one in the same position and to look for the best way to bring a solution to help salvage the issue. To judge that you be not judged would be, do unto others that which you would want to be done to you and those like you. There are times when we have no answer at hand, and we have to give it to the Powers that be and go with the flow.

Being a mother is the hardest job there is; it is also the most rewarding job there is. But at the end of the day, our children come through us, but they are not us, and they have their own journeys, their roads, and back streets to travel. In the next volume, I will show how there is no "poster mother"; as long as there is choice, there is opportunity for us to build or destroy, to clean or to deface. In other words, *to be or not to be* … is a question that only the individual can answer.

I leave you with Peace Love Health & Wealth …

—Akua Fayette

PS. The laws of attraction are already bringing people with "broken spirits" into my life. The beauty of it is God is preparing me to help. Not to accept pain and sorrow *from* them, but to guide them to finding their own way. In some cases, I am able to assist in situations where someone needs help. If I am able to step in and assist, this makes my day. When doing my duty and my work pays off not only for me but for others in my path, that is grace.

Imhotep's Spiritual Drummers by Akua

9

The "Gumbo" of Spiritual Healing

Dealing with "Broken" Children

Children are my main focus because of my own childhood. One of the gifts I received as a child was being able to analyze myself, as in Know Thyself. It is a gift that has kept me out of many sticky situations. Where I have faltered is when I try to analyze others; that is not really my business. I have learned in personal trials and situations that even when someone is in the wrong—and that does happen—my plan should be to check out *my* reaction, attitude, and emotions. In other words, do not take it personally, even sometimes when it really appears to be.

Children are great beings; if we take out the time to study them and study with them, while they are young, we can know this. But we spend so much time trying to mold, hush, put away, or overprotect them that we forget to sit back and observe them, ask them questions, and really listen.

I can hardly wait to start on HBS II, simply because we have only touched the surface of brokenness, when and how it begins. I have a friend in New York—her name is Joe Burrell—who has a definition on "What Is a Broken Spirit?" Her definition deals with babies that are unborn. I have stories of people from when they were babies in the womb and how they learned that their brokenness came from the emotional state of the mother at that time, especially where self-inflicted abortions were attempted and failed. Many of the definitions come from being broken as children, and that broken spirit follows into adulthood. She has a longer explanation that we will deal with in the next book, HBS II,

My painting, *Babies Wrapped in Gold* is my expression of how children are our greatest treasure. *The Three Sisters* painting is about the *village* of women and how three women can help to heal a community if they put all the things aside that keeps us away from peace, love, health, wealth, and happiness.

In this book, I have also highlighted brothers, but my focus is on showcasing sisters, who I feel will be our future history's heroes. I want to give them their flowers now, and in the next edition there will be more. *Who do we think has been given the position to carry such precious "cargo" to be birthed?* Answer: *Women.*

> *I believe if women* FOLLOW THEIR PURPOSE AND THEIR SPIRITS *we will have paved a way to love the world better, and the need for healing will be minimized.*
>
> —AF

> *Just remember it takes chaos …* BEFORE *the calm.*
>
> —AF

Waiting in the Car by Myself

Waiting in the car by myself,
Scared to call for someone to help.
Waiting on Mom or someone else …
I feel so hot, it seems like hell.
I want to get out, but I am by myself …
Where did they go, was it in the store?
Or in the bank? I want to thank you … if you should know …

Please hurry up, it's getting hot!
Why would they think it would be not?
The sun shines down, and the heat goes up …
I have had almost enough.
A baby has no way to say,
"Please let me out, it's hot today."

This is a car; it is not a place
To leave a child and let him stay.
So one more time, I have got to say,
It does not feel well.
Why should a child be left in a car
That feels like hell?

During an art class, I had the young people make cards for their parents, showing what it must be like to be a child in a hot car. One child drew a picture and wrote, "It feels like a hell hole!"

What could I say, being that such a travesty takes the lives of babies and young children every year? This is preventable, and it leads to broken spirits for the parents who unfortunately forgot or neglected a child, who they now have to hospitalize or bury. This is one way I use my symbolic art to change a mindset and help protect our children. Check your child; check your car!

Doors

Doors remind me of homes; every home has at least one.

As a child I was very connected to my community, and every home's door held a personality that dwelled behind it.

My original thought was to just paint the door abstractly, but I could not just stop at designs, being the symbolic artist I am.

One of the reasons you will see my name distinctly on my art is that the name Akua is my trademark, because of what it stands for … *Sweet Messeng*er. So whoever owns my art has a message of love and hope.

My mantra for this century is Peace, Love, Health, and Wealth.

I really believe that the healing of a community and the broken hearts of so many people can be healed by the unity of women from all cultures. The six women on the painted door named *DMT (Doing Miracles Together)* are united and surrounded by angelic wings of unity. The house in the painting represents the homes that need mending, and the cup and saucer represent the much-needed conversations for healing to take place. Most of all, the painting expresses the angelic love that can and does come from us when we join together—as mothers, sisters, wives, aunts, and friends. DMT … doing miracles together.

Setting the Record Straight

The one thing I want to make clear, if possible (though it really is not my *business* what people think), for the record, in case someone is wondering what I am, as in faith—Christian? Buddhist? Muslim? Jewish? or what? First of all I am, not I AM, but I am. As simple as that, I am a child of the Most High God of the Universe.

Credo

I believe in truth and that the laws of the universe are
for us, to guide our direction, but the choice is up
to us.
I believe what I put out, I will receive.

I appreciate truth from wherever I receive it.
I love the history and the life and the teachings of Jesus Christ, so am I Christian?
I love the rich culture and vision of the Jews, so am I Jewish?
I love the strength and discipline of the Muslim, so am I Muslim?
I love the Zen quality and the compassion of the Buddhist, so am I Buddhist?
I guess you could call me *BLESSED*—**b**eing **l**oved, **e**ngaged, **s**piritually **s**atisfied, **e**nduring **d**isappointments—and I am, still I am, and I am a child of the Most High.
I believe in the Golden Rule that is universal:
Do unto others as you would have them do to you.
Love is my true faith and the One that I follow.

Truly, I have been, during my life, the most faithful to one faith for thirty-two years, to the point I would have died for my belief. Now I realize that to keep an open mind allows me to learn and be available to truth when it comes knocking. Now I know one thing, as Master Chin would say, "God loves me, and I do no evil."

I respect everyone's right to their truth. This new way of living fills me with joy, as it places all responsibility *on me* for my life and my "salvation." I want to be the best of all these faiths that hold truth for me, for any law based on love is based on *the God Mind* … and let God be the judge in the end.

Last word about Our Mother …

Tomorrow, February 7, , will be the celebration of our dear mother's one hundredth birthday. We, all six surviving siblings, will be honoring her as we remember it did not matter how small the portion, or how much, she shared all that she had—except her cup of coffee and her Dove soap! And yes, she did have beautiful soft skin. We all miss her, and as I say to anyone who asks, her death seems like yesterday, for she is forever fresh in my heart and my mind, the one person who truly loved me. Better yet, she *understood* me. My dear mother, I never doubted her love for me or any of us.

I know that this truth has sent a message throughout the universe. It is time for fathers to know who their seeds are, just like mothers have the right. Why shouldn't DNA be a birthright, on the birth certificate, and made available to any man or woman to see if the child they have just received is of their DNA? So let the truth begin! *Love is the answer!*

Family Logo GOD FAMILY & COFFEE
Art by Albert Reff
(Art Work Creations)

Love Is the Oxygen of the Soul

The most beautiful thing in the world to behold
Is the beauty of love and what it does for the soul.
Love is a verb … so it must come with action …
Faith, belief, care, protect, share, and yes, some satisfaction.
For those who think sex is love … it is only an action
That can be laced with love or just human satisfaction.
You can't make love, so don't be deceived,
Love comes from physically and spiritually rolling up your sleeves.
It takes time and patience; it takes care and understanding.
Just buying and giving is not in the planning.
Yes, love is oxygen to the soul,
So relax, breathe easy, and give before it's gone.
The more you give, the more it grows,
So give that oxygen, and see it grow.
Give of that oxygen, and see it glow!
Like oxygen, we really do not live without love …
we merely exist … we barely feel the glow of life.
So please, breathe three times, and let love be the answer.

Dear Imhotep,

Words cannot express the beauty of being in love with someone that you prayed for at the age of ten.

We have had a long and exciting marriage, three brilliant children, wonderful grandchildren and grand-dogs. Like most people, we have had those moments of tests of disruption in relationships that caused one to wonder what would the next step be? … We have risen above the dust of doubt and disruption, for true love stands the test of time. As my soulmate, you have been my shoulder and the wings beneath my feet, and a few times the pebbles in my shoes. You have also been the one to bring out my deep inner weakness, which has made you my greatest asset, for no one alive could bring that side of me out but you. You know me inside out, but you also have not seen the best of me, which is yet to come. Even though the years have made their changes, as they do in our physical outfits, but the real me, the spirit within that is being healed on a daily basis, as I overcome me … *is the best you will ever experience in this lifetime.*

Upon writing a letter to my parents explaining how I felt and what I had learned and how much I appreciated the good and accepted the lessons of the unintentional mishaps in my childhood, It became clear to me that it has all been to my greater good.

I learned from writing a letter to Daddy that my love for you *has been* IGNITED *by the good times I witnessed with him with my mother when he was happy singing gospel songs or fixing things around the house or just talking and drinking coffee. This is where the Black Love and Coffee ritual we share comes from. But our remodeling also sparks that reminiscence of love and good times, as you have done more than your share.*

While I've been writing this book, you and I have been preparing our retirement home in our community, and it is the eighth house we have lived in in forty-six years together. The ninth house will be totally ready for us and will express the true understanding that we do not have to build it ourselves, it is already done. I want to see you in the light of your reward, which you so deserve for years of showing me you cared and giving me what I did not know was a symbol of love. I still have the wooden doll figure you cut out for me over thirty years ago.

Yes, we are soulmates, and we have shared the best of each other's talents, but what no one can see, the best is yet to come. Thanks for listening to me when I shared with you my greatest hurt as a child—and you always remembered not to forget. One of the best gifts you gave me was my name, for its meaning settled on my spirit and makes me remember to be humble and giving. As I was when I asked you, a little nervous, to give me a name, for I did not want to be presumptuous and name myself. You did a good job and made me proud that all my talking over the years left you with good feelings of my purpose to help others.

I have grown into "my big-girl emotional panties," and I can handle "being forgotten now." Matter of fact, at this stage and age of things, who really remembers well anyway? (smile) We have truly grown together and are still growing. . . .

Much love,
Akua
PLHW

Black Love and a Cup Of Coffee
Original painting by Akua

Forgive, Forgiven, Forgave

We all have met Forgiven.
We have been introduced to Forgave.
Until we forgive ourselves …
We will be "tangled in the webs we made."
So let's go deep with Iyanla and remove the layers of hurt.
Forgiving oneself is as important as a garden needs water and dirt.
Some will be so kind as to give the shirt from their back,
While not be willing to let go of the bad memories they pack.
Let's make our load much lighter
And forgive others and ourselves as we grow.
It's the greatest gift that keeps on giving
And brings joy and allows us to glow!

Peace Love Health and Wealth

This is the mantra I gave to myself,
Until I really understood truth.
My full experience would need some help.
Forgiving is a virtue, I thought.
It was easy for me to do.
What I found out that wasn't quite true.
Peace
Love
Health
Wealth:
I need the energy of all forgiveness and self-worth and help.
My peace love health and wealth has so much improved
As I forgive myself …

Forgiven

I have forgiven, that I know.
I have forgiven, that I have found.
I have forgiven now, more than I had.
But to forgive me is the best forgiving and makes me glad.
But I cannot be too bold to think that I have completed the task.
Forgiving is an ongoing exercise that must continue,
For every day or at least once in a while, my "ego" will take control,
And I once again have to forgive another soul.
But most of all, I must forgive myself.
And seek the wisdom and get the help …
Forgiveness is complex!

October of last year, I attended Oprah's tour, "The Life You Want Weekend." I had not gone on a vacation or taken a trip in ages. I had been working on several projects, redesigning a house on a special budget, finishing a book, and a number of other things, but I was told I would be receiving an e-mail from Oprah. And when one came through, I *knew* it was the thing to do.

It was fantastic. The only thing I purchased was Iyanla Vanzant's course "Forgiveness." This is the funny part: I took the course to be able to help others in forgiving, for I believed I had that covered, and I did partly, but once into the course, which was unbelievably phenomenal, I found I had, in many situations, not forgiven myself. I would recommend that that course be required in every school, every church, and in every public facility. It was priceless, and she made any review of the course an ongoing gift, so this little section of poetry is my tribute for the joy of finding my character's strength and weakness. Over the last four years or more, I had already learned that I needed to work on these things—to *do my duty.* So that made me feel good, to know for sure I was headed in the right direction. And then, being invited for one year to co-host at a local radio station proved to me—and others—that I had gained much strength in humility.

I always felt Oprah and I had so much in common. I want to thank Oprah for setting the greatest example of forgiveness and reconciliation between friends in public. That is what my art piece *The Three Sisters* is about, and I am doing a personal *Three Sisters* to remind me of the lessons that the two of you have taught me on forgiveness. Look what it has produced! You are both better than ever before in what each of you bring to the table of life!

Who says sisters don't know how to get along? Thanks.

Do Your Duty …

Says Master C with a grin.
He says it over and over again—
Do your duty.
Pray, and then he says it again.
Do your duty.
Eat right.
Do your duty.
Change your way of thinking.
Do your duty.
You will be blessed.
You will be healed.
You will grow wiser.
Yes … do *your* duty.
This is the engine of divine will.
Do your duty.
Remember: *be still, and know that I Am …*

To all members of the community not mentioned in these pages, thank you for your contributions in so many areas, such as prayers, kind words, and so on. And sometimes doing nothing is better than being a deterrent, and I was blessed to not have any deterrents, as far as I know. There are many relatives whom we do not even *know* but should know. There some we know who live here, but because of the "brokenness" that causes small epidemics in families to be disconnected (and even sometimes when one makes a move to heal the brokenness), failure sets in. But still, we must each "do our work" and "do our duty," as both Iyanla and Master C say.

I am ready and hope those distant loved ones are ready too.

By the way, I really don't know of a family without some dysfunctions. If you do, I would love to interview them! I love positive stories and solutions.

Yesterday would have been my dear mother's one hundredth birthday, and she would only have wanted to be here if she could take care of herself. All six siblings celebrated together in our old community, the one we grew up in, at the wonderful meeting room of a local organization. I have learned to live by this, and this is the reason it's been so hard to make out an acknowledgment list of all the people who helped me to be where I am today—because if the truth be known, it was the ones who emotionally or mentally abused or challenged me who made me work hardest to prove them wrong. So I do thank all who cross my path, for different reasons. Yet who doesn't love to be loved and appreciated? And those are the ones you celebrate life's goodness with; that's the difference. So this celebration is a new start for us to begin to heal and bring our families together.

And just in case anyone wants to know, writing this book was definitely not about money or ego; this book caused me to expose the one person who I love and will always love. And that wasn't easy.

Acknowledgement of Organizations, Businesses and Individuals

Over the last twenty-plus years of becoming free to be me, for the organizations, media, and businesses that made my work visible and my journey as successful as it has been—with more room to improve—I am ever grateful.

This list is to thank everyone be it in a big or small way, you touched my life.

This is how some of us celebrated President Obama's Inauguration Day: The Project Obama Clean .Paint. Plant, Celebration by SIPP (Sisters In Positive Progress), BIPP (Brothers In Positive Progress), South Park Pride Day—the first black president,

Special thanks to: Ester King., Ed Banks., Sandra Hines., other volunteers, and family members.

NBUF (National Black United Front)

Magic 102 (Ed Shannon's hour interview about NBUF and my first live reading of *Goose Sense* on-air)

Bel Park Civic Club (the community who supported my work)

African United for Sanity…

SHAPE Community Center

PBS New York, "Mom Documentary"

Special thanks to Louis Alvarez & Andy Kolker: www.CNMA.com

City of Houston's international book *Deep in the Heart of Houston* … (double-page spread of international exposure)

PBS Network Houston … Doris Childress

The Art Institute … (first exhibit "Women of Soul")

NBSA (National Black Social Workers of America)

KPFT Public Radio

KCOH Radio

KYSH Internet Radio

Black Heritage Society

Alpha Kappa Alpha Chapter commissioned art: *In My Mother's Shoes*

Imprint Inc. (book reading marathon)

Reginald Adams (MOCHA— my contact (Mom Documentary at PBS)

National Resource Center for Youth, University of Oklahoma (speaker)

Community Artist Collective, M. Barnes (guest speaker)

Museum of Fine Arts (exhibit of mini collection)

PHR (Project Row Houses) First Art /Gift Shop

Houston Area Urban League (art on display in New York office)

Houston Community College

Walt Disney Studios … (included in three weeks' exhibit "Black History")

Akelay King…. (*Goose Sense* children's book)

Minute Maid Awards (art contract) Angelia Cox

The Forward Times, Bernard Thibodaux (my first news article)

Texas Southern Library Dept., Dr. O. Kamau

T*he Houston Style* magazine (two-page spread)

The Defenders

The Houston Chronicle (a front-page article)

Southside Spotlight … "Akua's Korner" editorial

Charlie Bellinger, movie producer

Song Dog Records … Bill Ward … BLCC, CD

Children Are Our Future, Scholarship Gala (keynote speaker)

Citizen for Better Media JC & V. Young

Red Ink (my first movie, art credits)

Dr. Walls (contributions to community art classes)

Thomas and Taeta Malcom exhibiting Art at Texas Southern Univ.

KCOH—Michael Harris (promoted me for cohost and then host on KYSH)

Cush City Black Book Conference: Toastmaster

Mr. & Mrs. Goodrich, introducing GOOSE SENSE Children Story at Jowell Elementary

I Hunter III… framing, CD marketing and advertising.

C. R. Hunter …..Package Designer and Organizer

JIMBO (Kanara design) and wood stools

Yvonne Ross Fashion Design & Start-up Retail Manager

Elvenyia (my first great bio)

Edwina and Janice (Angelia's three-sister contribution)

Algenita Davis of Habitat for Humanity (honored the artists' beautiful art medal and gala of art doors fundraiser; DMT poem in book)

Dr. Joan Edwards (my first storytelling job that paid)

Houston Public Libraries, Scott St. and Downtown, Center for the Healing of Racism (first public intro of HBS)

Deloyd Parker … (took *Three Sisters* to Ghana)

Starbucks Art and Poetry performance

Borders Book Store (now gone)

Whole Foods (donated food for our cleanup crew)

The Married Ladies Club

Cleveland Lee first supported of SIPP

Celebrating Our Heritage and Our Land ... Mexia, Texas, 2014 (art poster)

New Orleans connections

Dallas connections

Austin connections

Atlanta Georgia connections

Washington, DC, connections

California connections

Tennessee connections

Florida connections

New York connections

Finished with much love and admiration for the community that thrives, because we know that we have worth and value, as all people are one in the lesson of life.

> *We all bleed and we all need, but to add to that, we must let our spirits feed from God's Universal Laws of Truth!*
>
> —AF

A Personal Promise

Many times Female elders are called Queens.
I am called that, on many occasions
I made a promise over five years ago,
that I would not use that
Title until
I wrote my first book to
Share my life's story
I have met the
challenge.
Yours humbly

Queen Akua

Miracle "Whip" being cool for bike ride
Photo by Akua

2nd oil painting at age 26
“Three Geese” by Akua

1st oil painting at age 26
Dark African Night

Family Wall Mural painting in progress
by Akua

Painting (Impressionist)
The Greatest Teacher
by Akua (from historical photo)

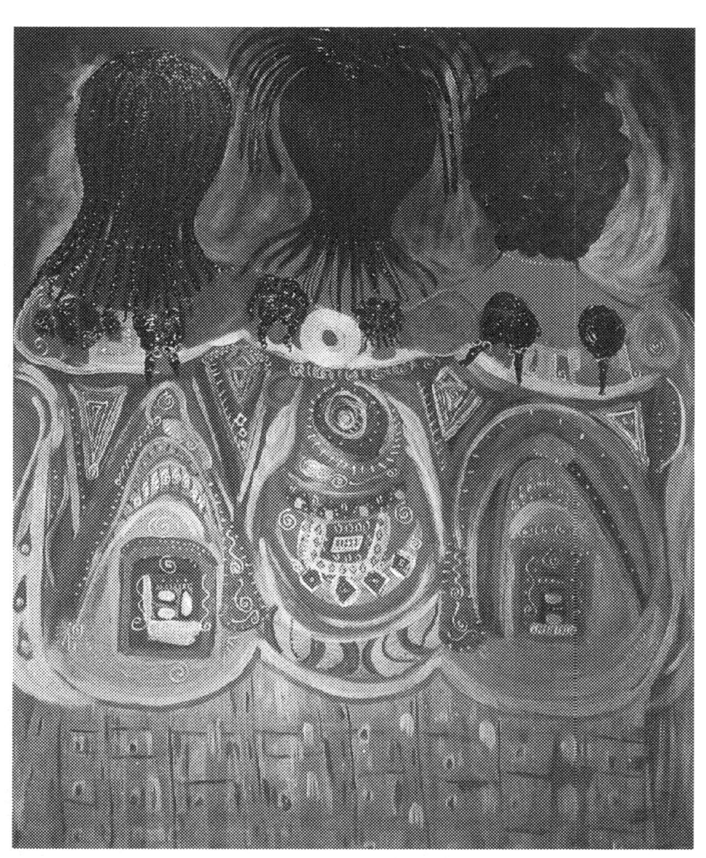

Chrystal's Guarding Our Girls
by Akua

Celebrating Our Heritage and Our land
Mexia Texas June 19 2013
Poster Art by Akua

Large bowl art
Mother and Child in Gold…
by Akua

1 of 6 Row Art Collection
By Akua

Wheeler Ave. Church Lady
Project art by 21 Church Women and Akua

First doodle pen and ink
"Three Geese" by Akua

Family art by Akua
"IN A ME" footstool by Jimbo

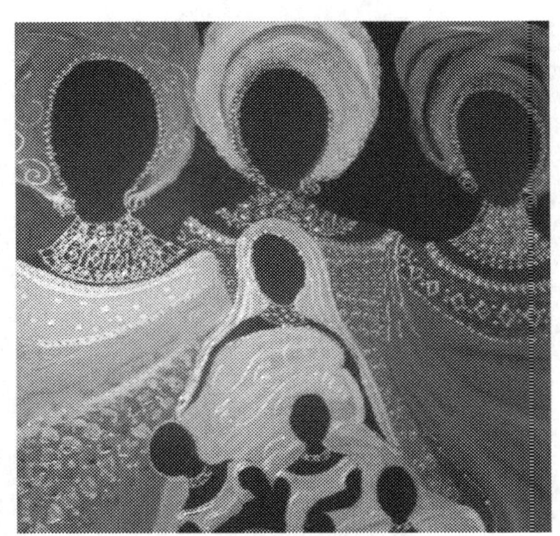

Wrapping Our babies in Gold
by Akua

"Broken Woman"
Becomes whole by Akua

Chrystal's Black Love and a Cup of Chocolate by Akua

Exhibit SWHCC Sculpture painted baby evolving in gold by Akua

Brass tray: Storyteller in Town by Akua

Libation stand made by Imhotep Designed and painted by Akua

First copy of first painting of Mother and Child by Akua

The Story-Teller brass tray, and the Stump People

SouthWest Community College Gallery
Akua Fayette One Woman Art Exhbit February 2013

LET'S DO IT AGAIN (' - ') !!!!!!!!!!

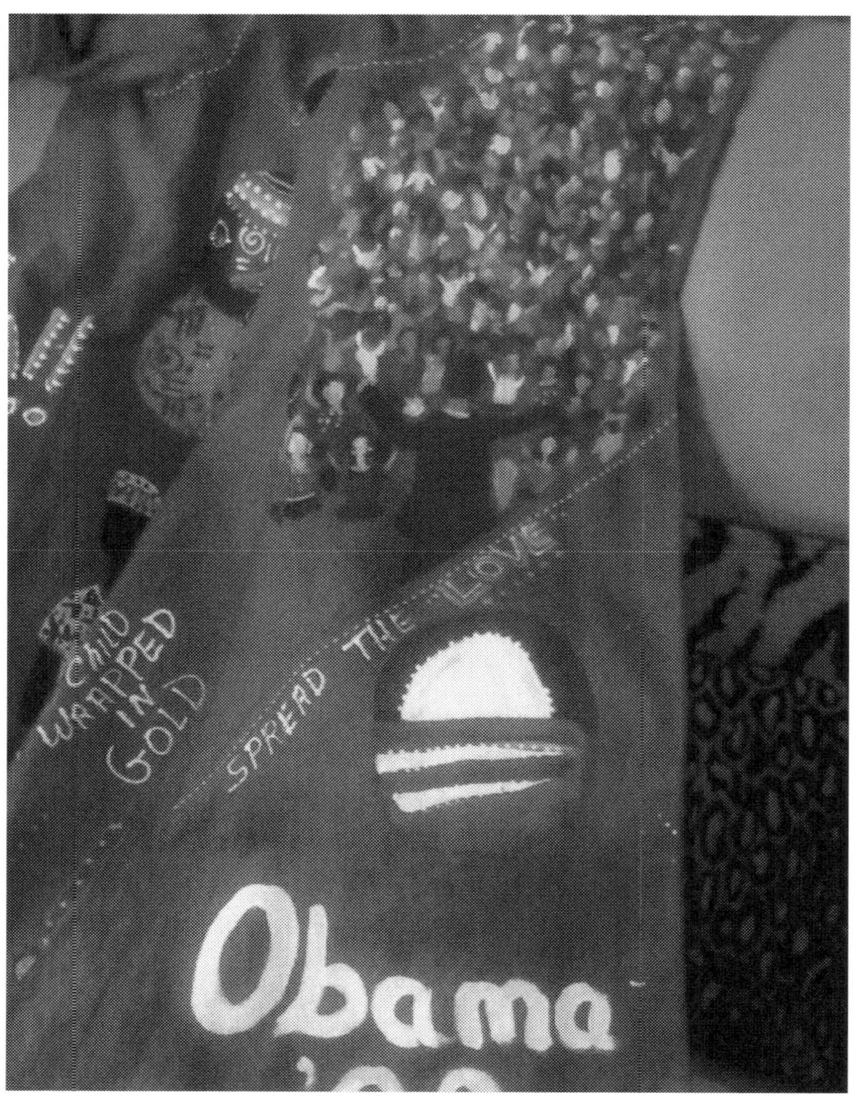

Hand painted Dress coat
By Akua to wear
"If Obama Won" and yes He did!

Special Dedication

Yvonne Cassandra Francis

In memory of my niece, Sandy as we fondly called her began to work with me in organizing my little personal library

During her treatment for cancer, between the times when the pain was not so great, she would sat and organize my book collection.

We talked about her traveling with me as my assistant to my book signing as she herself was writing a book. A compassionate loving young lady who was gentle in her mannerism and was a loving niece to me and a loving daughter to my sister, her mother of whom she was named after. She leaves behind four brothers as she was the only girl. She will be greatly missed, yet her spirit will fill the air wherever I am on my book tours. She was braved and never gave up hope. She participated in the definition of what is a broken spirit? Her spirit was one of love and hope and she is and will always be my sweet niece.

Sandy left us July 29 2015…..but will be with us in mind and spirit.

There will be a Women Inspirational Book Club in her honor starting September this year.

Words of Love and Wisdom came from my oldest sister Bettye D., She did not want to be a bother as she was strong willed and independent, We will miss her smile and laughter…I did get a chance to get her input into this book which was finished when she passed. The Healing of a Broken Spirit has prepared me for the lost of two love ones…in Healing of Broken Spirit II. I will be able to express my experience in how this book has changed my life.

Printed in the United States
By Bookmasters